Plastic Canvas
Bazaar Bestsellers™

the Needlecraft Shop

Plastic Canvas Bazaar Bestsellers™

Editor	Cathy Mullins
Art Director	Brad Snow
Publishing Services Director	Brenda Gallmeyer
Managing Editor	Dianne Schmidt
Assistant Art Director	Nick Pierce
Copy Supervisor	Michelle Beck
Copy Editors	Mary O'Donnell
	Susanna Tobias
Technical Editor	June Sprunger
Graphic Production Supervisor	Ronda Bechinski
Graphic Artists	Debby Keel
	Edith Teegarden
Production Assistants	Marj Morgan
	Judy Neuenschwander
Photography Supervisor	Tammy Christian
Photography	Don Clark
	Matthew Owen
Photo Stylist	Tammy Steiner
Chief Executive Officer	David McKee
Book Marketing Director	Dwight Seward

Printed in China
First Printing: 2008
Library of Congress Control Number: 2007941953
Hardcover ISBN: 978-1-57367-292-4
Softcover ISBN: 978-1-57367-308-2

Every effort has been made to ensure the accuracy and completeness of the instructions in this book. However, we cannot be responsible for human error or for the results when using materials other than those specified in the instructions, or for variations in individual work.

DRGbooks.com

1 2 3 4 5 6 7 8 9

Welcome!

We all have memories of craft bazaars growing up. Yours may have been at the county fair or a special fundraising event for your church, civic group or school, but the experience was the same—that of a community coming together to showcase the beautiful handiwork of local crafters. There was always a wonderful variety of items to choose from, and the experience was unforgettable.

We have filled this book with a delightful assortment of projects that will recreate that bazaar experience as well as give you some great home decor and gift-giving ideas. From tissue toppers to coaster sets to photo frames, you're sure to find lots of projects that will fit your needs! There are quick-to-stitch items that can be made in a day or less. Included are designs to display year-round as well as decorations for Christmas, Halloween, Thanksgiving and Easter.

We hope you enjoy stitching these great designs for your next bazaar, as gifts for loved ones, and of course, for yourself!

Happy Stitching!

Cathy Mullins

Year-Round Bazaar

4

Designs to Make in a Day

Holiday Bazaar

5

Year-Round Bazaar

Delightful for year-round decorating, this chapter is chock-full of designs you'll love to stitch. Perfect to sell at bazaars or to give as gifts, there's something for everyone!

Kitty Tissue Holder

Cute and cuddly, this kitty tissue holder is sized to fit in your vehicle's cup holder.

Design by Debra Arch

SKILL LEVEL
Intermediate

SIZE
7½ inches H x 3¼ inches in diameter (19.1cm x 8.3cm)

MATERIALS
- 1 sheet clear 7-count plastic canvas
- Small amount white 7-count plastic canvas
- 2 (3-inch) Uniek QuickShape plastic canvas radial circles
- Red Heart Plush medium weight yarn Art. E719 as listed in color key
- Kreinik ⅛-inch Ribbon as listed in color key
- #16 tapestry needle
- 2 (8mm) round black beads
- Rose blush and cotton swab (optional)
- Hot-glue gun

PROJECT NOTE
Use 2 strands when stitching with yarn and 1 strand when stitching with ribbon unless otherwise instructed.

INSTRUCTIONS
1. Cut top and base from 3-inch radial circles (page 10), cutting away gray areas. Cut whiskers from white plastic canvas according to graph (page 10), cutting away blue lines. Base and whiskers will remain unstitched.

2. Cut body, tail front, ears and nose from clear plastic canvas according to graphs (pages 10 and 11). Cut one 56-hole x 29-hole piece from clear for base side. Base side will remain unstitched.

3. Stitch body and tail front following graphs, leaving bottom portion of tail unstitched as indicated. When background stitching is completed, work Straight Stitches on paws with 1 strand apricot.

4. Matching edges, Whipstitch tail front to tail on body from arrow to arrow. Using apricot, tack left edge of tail front from arrow to blue dot to inside of body.

5. Whipstitch side edges of body and remaining edge of tail together, working through all three layers and forming back seam.

6. Overcast inside edge of top, then Whipstitch outside edge to top edge of body, carefully working across edge in front of tail.

7. Using apricot, Whipstitch side edges of base side together, then Whipstitch bottom edge to outside edge of base.

8. For ear front pieces, stitch one as graphed; reverse one before stitching. Repeat for ear back pieces, replacing white with apricot. Matching edges, Whipstitch ear front and back pieces together.

9. Stitch and Overcast nose.

ASSEMBLY
1. Using photo as a guide throughout assembly, glue ears in place on top.

2. Arrange whiskers so one end on each is inside blue placement lines for nose. Glue ends in place, then glue nose over whiskers.

3. Glue beads for eyes where indicated on graph.

4. For hair tuft, wrap 1 strand of apricot around three fingers five times. Remove from fingers and tie in center with another length of apricot. Cut loops open to form tuft. Glue to top of head where indicated on graph.

5. If desired, add blush to cheeks with cotton swab.

6. Gently roll a stack of 10 pop-up tissues from one short end to the other, keeping center tissue up enough to pull out.

7. Insert tissues into base with pull out tissue at open end. Slide kitty over base, pulling center tissue through opening in top.

8. To refill, insert finger into opening in base, then gently pull base from kitty and repeat steps 6 and 7. •

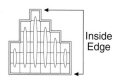

**Kitty Tissue Holder
Ear Front & Back**
6 holes x 6 holes
Cut 2, reverse 1, from
clear for fronts
Stitch as graphed
Cut 2, reverse 1, from
clear for backs
Stitch with apricot

Inside
Edge

**Kitty Tissue Holder
Nose**
5 holes x 3 holes
Cut 1 from clear

10

COLOR KEY

Yards	Medium Weight Yarn
10 (9.2m)	☐ White #9001 (2 strands)
60 (54.9m)	☐ Apricot #9220 (2 strands)
	✎ Apricot #9220 (1-strand) Straight Stitch
	◉ Attach apricot #9220 hair tuft
1 (1m)	
	⅛-Inch Ribbon
	☐ Star pink #092
	● Attach bead

Color numbers given are for Red Heart Plush
medium weight yarn Art. E719 and Kreinik
⅛-inch Ribbon.

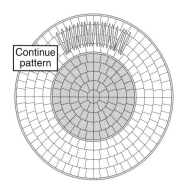

**Kitty Tissue Holder
Whisker**
7 holes x 7 holes
Cut 6 from white,
cutting away blue lines

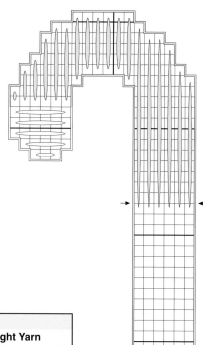

Do not
stitch

**Kitty Tissue Holder
Tail Front**
18 holes x 51 holes
Cut 1 from clear

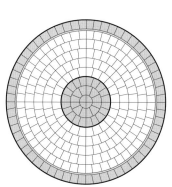

Continue
pattern

Kitty Tissue Holder Top
Cut 1 from radial circle,
cutting away gray area

Kitty Tissue Holder Base
Cut 1 from radial circle,
cutting away gray area
Do not stitch

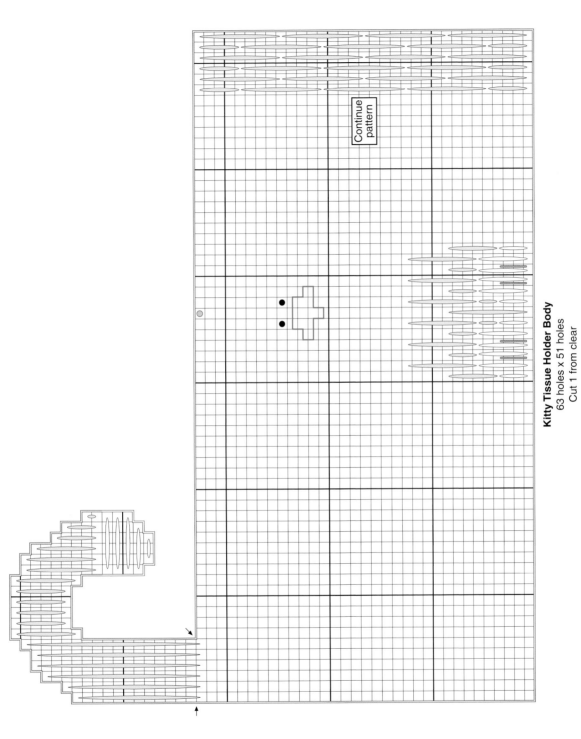

Kitty Tissue Holder Body
63 holes x 51 holes
Cut 1 from clear

Continue pattern

11

Cat Lover's Bookend

Cat lovers will delight in this tiger kitty bookend.

Design by Alida Macor

INSTRUCTIONS

1. Cut plastic canvas according to graph. Back will remain unstitched. Cut felt one hole smaller all around than cat.

2. Stitch front following graph. When background stitching is completed, work black pearl cotton Backstitches and Straight Stitches.

3. Adhere felt to back of stitched cat, making sure to leave room for stitching edges.

4. Using black yarn throughout, Overcast bottom edge of front. Whipstitch front and back together around side and top edges.

Note: *To completely cover edges, it may be necessary to take two stitches in every other hole.*

5. Slide stitched cat shape over metal bookend. •

SKILL LEVEL
Beginner

SIZE
5⅛ inches W x 6¼ inches H (13cm x 15.9cm)

MATERIALS
- ½ sheet 7-count plastic canvas
- Medium weight yarn as listed in color key
- #3 pearl cotton as listed in color key
- #16 tapestry needle
- 5-inch/12.7cm-high black metal bookend
- White self-adhesive felt

12

COLOR KEY	
Yards	**Medium Weight Yarn**
7 (6.5m)	■ Black
7 (6.5m)	□ White
6 (5.5m)	▨ Light rust
4 (3.7m)	▨ Rust
1 (1m)	▨ Light green
1 (1m)	□ Pink
	#3 Pearl Cotton
2 (1.9m)	╱ Black Backstitch and Straight Stitch

Cat Lover's Bookend Front & Back
33 holes x 40 holes
Cut 2
Stitch front only

Doghouse Coaster Set

Have a doggone good time with this fun coaster set that's for more than the dogs!

Designs by Deborah Scheblein

INSTRUCTIONS

1. Cut plastic canvas according to graphs (pages 16 and 17). Cut brown felt to fit coasters.

2. Stitch and Overcast coasters following graphs, working uncoded areas with white Continental Stitches. Glue felt to back of each coaster.

3. Stitch doghouse front, back, sides and base following graphs, working uncoded areas on front with brown Continental Stitches.

4. Using red, Whipstitch front and back to sides, then Whipstitch front, back and sides to base. Overcast roof edges with brown and top edges of sides and back with red.

5. Stitch and Overcast sign, bowl, grass, and dog front, back and muzzle following graphs, working uncoded background on sign with ecru Continental Stitches.

6. When background stitching is completed, work brown Backstitches for letters on sign.

7. Using photo as a guide, center and glue dog front to dog back, making sure bottom edges are even. Glue muzzle to dog front where indicated on graph with blue lines.

8. Glue cabochons to head for eyes and pompom to muzzle for nose where indicated on graphs.

9. Using photo as a guide, glue dog and bowl to doghouse front, making sure bottom edges are even. Glue sign over door. Center and glue grass to back, making sure bottom edges are even. •

SKILL LEVEL
Beginner

SIZES
Coasters: 4¼ inches W x 3¾ inches H (10.8cm x 9.5cm)

Doghouse Holder: 6 inches W x 5¾ inches H x 2¼ inches D (15.2cm x 14.6cm x 5.7cm)

MATERIALS
- 1½ sheets 7-count plastic canvas
- Medium weight yarn as listed in color key
- #16 tapestry needle
- 2 (6mm) round black cabochons
- 7mm black pompom
- Brown felt
- Hot-glue gun

14

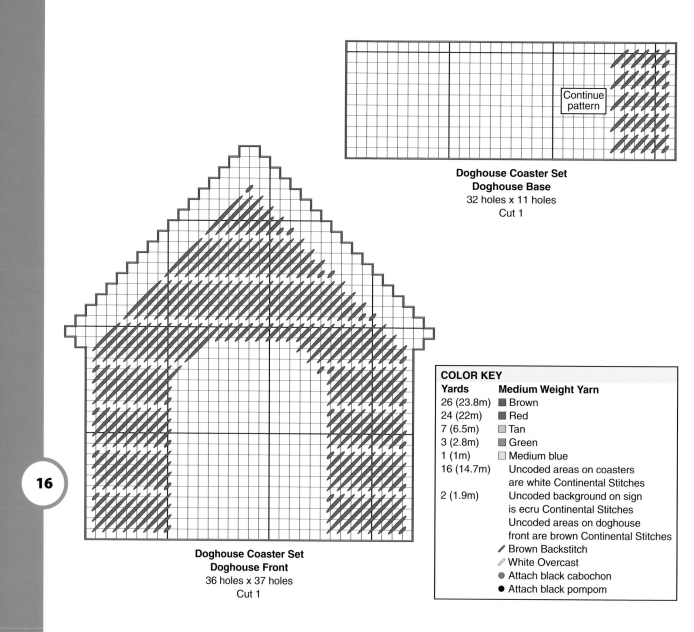

Doghouse Coaster Set
Doghouse Base
32 holes x 11 holes
Cut 1

Doghouse Coaster Set
Doghouse Front
36 holes x 37 holes
Cut 1

COLOR KEY

Yards	Medium Weight Yarn
26 (23.8m)	■ Brown
24 (22m)	■ Red
7 (6.5m)	□ Tan
3 (2.8m)	■ Green
1 (1m)	□ Medium blue
16 (14.7m)	Uncoded areas on coasters are white Continental Stitches
2 (1.9m)	Uncoded background on sign is ecru Continental Stitches
	Uncoded areas on doghouse front are brown Continental Stitches
	╱ Brown Backstitch
	╱ White Overcast
	● Attach black cabochon
	● Attach black pompom

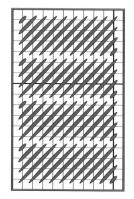

Doghouse Coaster Set
Doghouse Side
11 holes x 17 holes
Cut 2

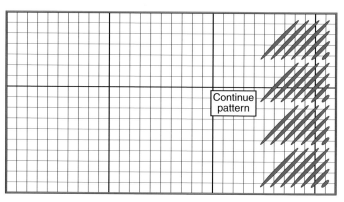

Doghouse Coaster Set
Doghouse Back
32 holes x 17 holes
Cut 1

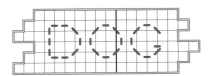

Doghouse Coaster Set Sign
18 holes x 6 holes
Cut 1

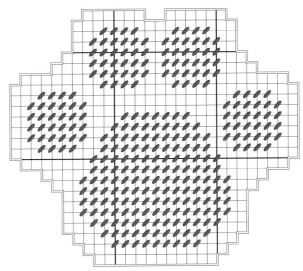

Doghouse Coaster Set Coaster
28 holes x 24 holes
Cut 4

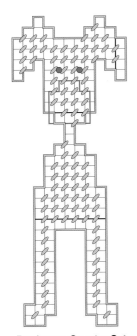

Doghouse Coaster Set Dog Front
11 holes x 29 holes
Cut 1

Doghouse Coaster Set Dog Muzzle
4 holes x 4 holes
Cut 1

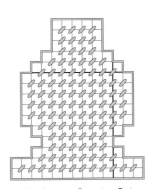

Doghouse Coaster Set Dog Back
13 holes x 15 holes
Cut 1

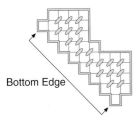

Bottom Edge

Doghouse Coaster Set Dog Bowl
9 holes x 9 holes
Cut 1

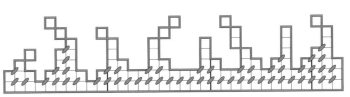

Doghouse Coaster Set Grass
33 holes x 7 holes
Cut 1

17

Sunflower Desk Set

Dress up your desk with a pretty sunflower mouse pad and matching coaster. Your desk has never looked so nice!

Designs by Cynthia Roberts

INSTRUCTIONS

1. Cut plastic canvas according to graphs (this page and page 53).
2. Stitch and Overcast pieces following graphs, working uncoded areas on white background with black Continental Stitches and uncoded areas on yellow background with yellow Continental Stitches.
3. If desired, cut felt to fit coaster and mouse pad. Adhere to back sides. •

GRAPHS CONTINUED ON PAGE 53

18

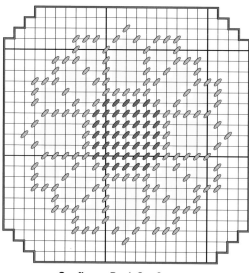

Sunflower Desk Set Coaster
24 holes x 24 holes
Cut 1

COLOR KEY	
Yards	**Medium Weight Yarn**
5 (4.6m)	■ Red
4 (3.7m)	■ Green
4 (3.7m)	■ Gold
2 (1.9m)	■ Dark brown
26 (23.8m)	Uncoded areas on white background are black Continental Stitches
4 (3.7m)	Uncoded areas on yellow background are yellow Continental Stitches
✀ Black Overcast	

Gerbera Daisy Cube

Bright and funky, this colorful cube will jazz up any space in your home.

Design by Kathy Wirth

INSTRUCTIONS

1. Cut four sides and one base from plastic canvas according to graph. Base will remain unstitched.

2. Stitch sides following graph, working uncoded areas with white Continental Stitches.

3. Using yellow throughout, Whipstitch sides together, then Whipstitch sides to unstitched base. Overcast top edges.

4. Apply glue to plastic foam sides, then insert into stitched cube.

5. Cut flower stem to about 7 inches (17.8cm). Insert in center of foam cube. Curve stem slightly.

6. Glue moss to foam, covering top. •

SKILL LEVEL
Beginner

SIZE
3½ inches W x 3½ inches H x 3½ inches D (8.9cm x 8.9cm x 8.9cm), excluding daisy

MATERIALS
- 1 sheet stiff 7-count plastic canvas
- Red Heart Classic medium weight yarn Art. E267 as listed in color key
- Red Heart Super Saver medium weight yarn Art. E301 as listed in color key
- Red Heart Kids medium weight yarn Art. E711 as listed in color key
- #16 tapestry needle
- 3-inch (7.6cm) white plastic foam cube
- Floral sheet moss
- Silk gerbera daisy
- Hot-glue gun

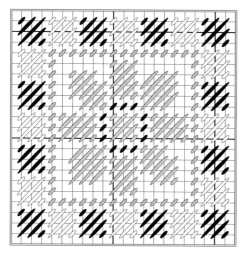

Gerbera Daisy Cube Side & Base
22 holes x 22 holes
Cut 5, stitch 4

COLOR KEY	
Yards	**Medium Weight Yarn**
12 (11m)	☐ White #1
9 (8.3m)	■ Black #12
5 (4.6m)	☐ Hot pink #727
4 (3.7m)	☐ Yellow #2230
6 (5.5m)	☐ Lime #2652
	Uncoded areas are white #1 Continental Stitches

Color numbers given are for Red Heart Classic medium weight yarn Art. E267, Super Saver medium weight yarn Art. E301 and Kids medium weight yarn Art. E711.

Blue Skies Frame

Sized for a 5 x 7-inch acrylic frame, this colorful frame cover is perfect for showcasing your summertime snapshots.

Design by Gina Woods

INSTRUCTIONS

1. Cut plastic canvas according to graphs (this page and page 54), cutting away gray area on radial circle.

2. Stitch and Overcast pieces following graphs, working cloud with white French Knots.

3. Using photo as a guide, hot-glue cloud to rainbow, then glue rainbow to upper right corner of stitched frame.

4. Using flexible, gap-filling glue throughout, attach stitched frame to front of acrylic frame. Glue button to lower left corner. •

GRAPHS CONTINUED ON PAGE 54

SKILL LEVEL
Beginner

SIZE
5⅝ inches W x 7⅛ inches H (14.3cm x 18.1cm)

MATERIALS
- ⅓ sheet 7-count plastic canvas
- 3-inch (7.6cm) plastic canvas radial circle
- Medium weight yarn as listed in color key
- #16 tapestry needle
- ¾-inch (1.9cm) novelty button (sample used blue star)
- Elmer's Stix-All flexible, gap-filling glue
- Hot-glue gun

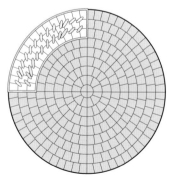

Blue Skies Frame Rainbow
Cut 1 from 3-inch radial circle,
cutting away gray area

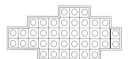

**Blue Skies Frame
Cloud**
11 holes x 5 holes
Cut 1

COLOR KEY	
Yards	**Medium Weight Yarn**
7 (6.5m)	■ Cornflower blue
3 (2.8m)	■ Light aqua
2 (1.9m)	□ Orchid
1 (1m)	□ Light blue
1 (1m)	□ Light yellow
1 (1m)	□ Spring green
2 (1.9m)	⁄ White Overcast
1 (1m)	⁄ Pink Overcast
	○ White French Knot

22

Beach Umbrellas Frame

Display your favorite "at the beach" photos in an acrylic frame covered with a stitched scene. This piece can also be adhered to a 12 x 12-inch album for a fun cover.

Design by Gina Woods

INSTRUCTIONS

1. Cut one beach scene and 16 umbrella hearts from plastic canvas according to graphs (pages 25 and 55).

2. Cut four 1½-inch (3.8cm) circles and four ½-inch (1.3cm) squares from 2mm white craft foam.

3. Stitch and Overcast pieces following graphs, working four hearts for one umbrella with red and white as graphed. Stitch four each for remaining umbrellas replacing red with royal blue, dark pink and orange.

4. For each umbrella, center and hot glue one craft foam square on top of one craft foam circle.

5. Arrange each set of umbrella hearts over a craft foam assembly, covering circle and placing points at center with sides in brackets touching. Hot-glue in place to form a slightly dimensional dome. Use flexible, gap-filling glue to attach one bead to top of each umbrella.

6. Using photo as a guide through step 7, arrange and hot-glue umbrellas on sand (tan section).

7. Using flexible, gap-filling glue through step 8, attach starfish and fish buttons to beach scene where indicated on graph.

8. Glue beach scene to one side of acrylic frame. •

GRAPHS CONTINUED ON PAGE 55

SKILL LEVEL
Beginner

SIZE
8 inches W x 10 inches H (20.3cm x 25.4m)

MATERIALS
- 1 sheet 7-count plastic canvas
- Medium weight yarn as listed in color key
- Metallic craft cord as listed in color key
- #16 tapestry needle
- Buttons:
    2 (⅝-inch/1.6cm) starfish
    3 (⅝-inch/1.6cm) blue fish
- 4 (6mm) brown transparent faceted beads
- Small amount 2mm white craft foam
- 8 x 10-inch (20.3 x 25.4cm) double vertical acrylic frame
- Elmer's Stix-All flexible, gap-filling glue
- Hot-glue gun

24

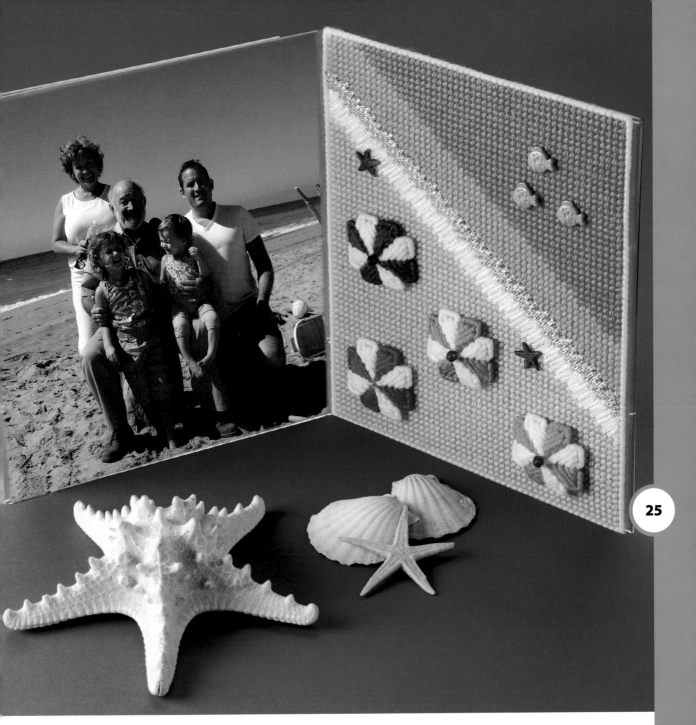

COLOR KEY

Yards	Medium Weight Yarn
29 (27.5m)	☐ Tan
24 (22m)	▨ Aqua
15 (13.8m)	☐ Light aqua
4 (3.7m)	☐ White
1 (1m)	■ Red
1 (1m)	Dark royal
1 (1m)	Dark pink
1 (1m)	Orange
4 (3.7m)	✏ Light pink Overcast
	Metallic Craft Cord
6 (5.5m)	☐ White pearl
4 (3.7m)	☐ Blue iridescent
	★ Attach starfish button
	● Attach blue fish button

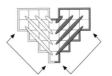

**Beach Umbrellas Frame
Umbrella Heart**
7 holes x 5 holes
Cut 16
Stitch 4 as graphed
Stitch 4 each replacing
red with royal blue,
dark pink and orange

Celtic Coasters

The luck of the Irish abounds with these pretty Celtic-inspired coasters. They're perfect for St. Paddy's Day or year-round!

Design by Terry Ricioli

INSTRUCTIONS

1. Cut plastic canvas according to graphs.

2. Following graphs throughout, stitch and Overcast coasters. Stitch holder base and holder corners, keeping stitching as neat as possible on backs of corner pieces.

3. Using holly throughout and with wrong sides facing, Whipstitch corner edges of each corner set together. With holder base facing up, Whipstitch corners to base. Overcast all remaining edges. •

SKILL LEVEL
Beginner

SIZES
Coasters: 3¾ inches square (9.5cm)

Coaster Holder: 4 inches square x 1⅝ inches H (10.2cm x 4.1cm)

MATERIALS
- 1 sheet 7-count plastic canvas
- Uniek Needloft plastic canvas yarn as listed in color key
- #16 tapestry needle

26

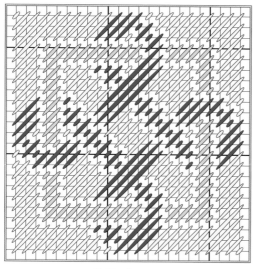

Celtic Coaster
24 holes x 24 holes
Cut 4

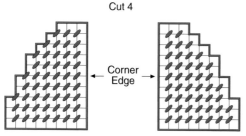

← Corner Edge →

Celtic Coasters Corner
8 holes x 10 holes each
Cut 4 sets

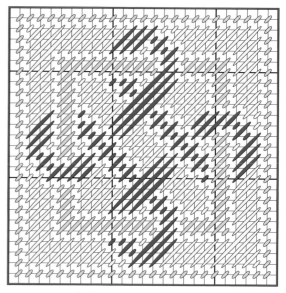

Celtic Coasters Holder Base
26 holes x 26 holes
Cut 1

COLOR KEY	
Yards	**Plastic Canvas Yarn**
23 (21.1m)	■ Holly #27
15 (13.8m)	□ Eggshell #39
15 (13.8m)	▨ Mermaid #53
Color numbers given are for Uniek Needloft plastic canvas yarn.	

Baby Bear Ornaments

Welcome a newborn with a darling baby bear ornament. Pick from a boy or girl baby bear design.

Designs by Rhonda Bryce

INSTRUCTIONS

1. Cut plastic canvas according to graphs (pages 30 and 31), cutting away gray area on radial circles.

2. Stitch and Overcast circles following graph, using baby print multicolored yarn.

3. Stitch and Overcast boy baby bear following graph, working uncoded areas with bronze Continental Stitches. Stitch and Overcast girl baby bear, replacing bronze with coffee and light blue with petal pink.

4. When background stitching is completed, work black Straight Stitches above muzzle on each bear and pink Backstitches for mouths.

5. Use photo as a guide through step 8. Using hand-sewing needle and bronze thread, stitch boy baby bear head, hands and feet to one circle. Repeat with girl baby bear and remaining circle, using dark brown thread.

6. Using hand-sewing needle and blue thread, stitch rattle button to one hand on boy baby bear and blue bear next to one foot.

7. Using hand-sewing needle and pink thread, stitch diaper pin button to top center of diaper on girl baby bear and rattle button to one hand.

8. For hangers, using light blue ribbon for boy baby and light pink ribbon for girl baby, thread ends of ribbon from front to back through holes indicated on corresponding radial circles; knot ends on back side. •

SKILL LEVEL
Beginner

SIZE
5⅞ inches in diameter (15cm), excluding hanger

MATERIALS
Each
- ½ sheet 7-count plastic canvas
- 6-inch Uniek QuickShape plastic canvas radial circle
- Red Heart Classic medium weight yarn Art. E267 as listed in color key
- Red Heart Super Saver medium weight yarn Art. E300 as listed in color key
- Red Heart Super Saver medium weight yarn Art. E301 as listed in color key
- #16 tapestry needle
- Hand-sewing needle

Boy Baby
- Favorite Findings It's a Boy! #550000001 rattle and blue bear buttons from Blumenthal Lansing Co.
- ¼ yard (0.2m) ¼-inch/7mm-wide light blue satin ribbon
- Blue and bronze thread

Girl Baby
  Favorite Findings It's a Girl! #550000002 rattle and diaper pin buttons from Blumenthal Lansing Co.
- ¼ yard (0.2m) ¼-inch/7mm-wide light pink satin ribbon
- Pink and dark brown thread

28

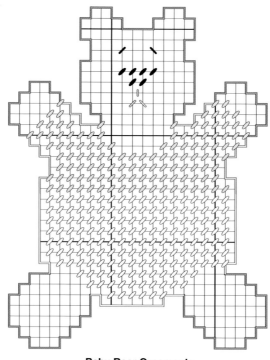

Baby Bear Ornaments
Baby Bear
25 holes x 32 holes
Cut 1 for boy baby bear
Stitch as graphed
Cut 1 for girl baby bear
Stitch replacing bronze with coffee
and light blue with petal pink

COLOR KEY	
Yards	**Medium Weight Yarn**
10 (9.2m)	☐ White #311
1 (1m)	■ Black #312
14 (12.9m)	☐ Baby print #345
4 (3.7m)	Petal pink #373
4 (3.7m)	☐ Light blue #381
6 (5.5m)	Uncoded areas on boy bear are bronze #286 Continental Stitches
6 (5.5m)	Uncoded areas on girl bear are coffee #365 Continental Stitches
╱	Bronze #286 Overcast
╱	Black #312 Straight Stitch
╱	Petal pink #373 Backstitch
●	Attach ribbon hanger

Color numbers given are for Red Heart Classic medium weight yarn Art. E267 and Super Saver medium weight yarn Art. E300 and Art. E301.

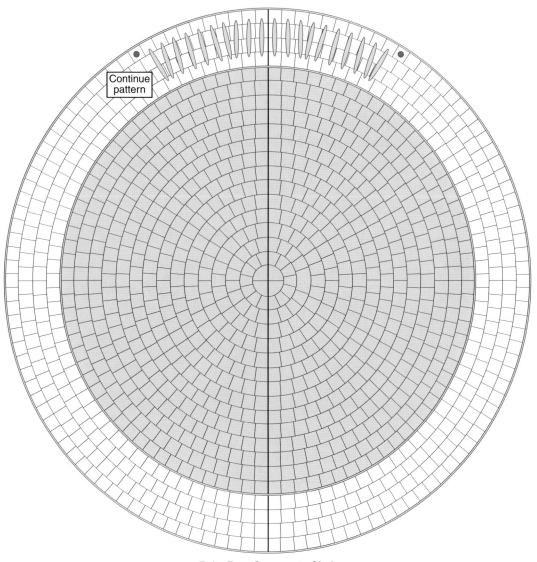

Baby Bear Ornaments Circle
Cut 1 for each ornament
from 6-inch radial circle

Flower Frames

Precut shapes make these tiny frames a snap to create. Bright colors and tiny embellishments add flair!

Designs by Rhonda Bryce

INSTRUCTIONS

Photo Holder

1. For each frame, cut one 4-inch plastic canvas radial circle in half along straight bar. Photo holders will remain unstitched.

Rainbow Flower Frame

1. Cut frame from 4-inch radial circle and petals from 3-inch radial circle according to graphs (page 34), cutting away gray areas.
2. Stitch and Overcast frame and petals following graphs, leaving center area and straight edge of petals unstitched.
3. Using photo as a guide through step 5 and using hand-sewing needle and orange thread through step 4, overlap and stitch petals around back of frame, making sure unstitched areas on petals do not show.
4. Place photo holder behind petals, centered over bottom half of frame, with straight edge behind opening; Whipstitch in place.
5. Using hand-sewing needle and green thread, sew shamrock buttons to frame.
6. For hanging loop, attach a small length Christmas green yarn behind petals.

Pastel Flower Frame

1. Cut frame from 4-inch radial circle and petals from 3-inch radial circle according to graphs (page 35), cutting away gray areas.
2. Following graphs throughout, Stitch and Overcast frame. Stitch and Overcast one petal with petal pink as graphed, leaving straight edge unstitched. Repeat with remaining petals, stitching one each with cornmeal, light mint, light blue and lavender.
3. Using photo as a guide and using hand-sewing needle and off-white thread through step 5, overlap and stitch petals around back of frame.
4. Center and stitch white ribbon rose to light mint petal. Stitch remaining ribbon roses to petals with matching color shade.
5. Place photo holder behind petals, centered over bottom half of frame, with straight edge behind opening; Whipstitch in place.
6. For hanging loop, attach a small length of matching yarn behind petals.

Denim Flower Frame

1. Cut frame from 4-inch radial circle and petals from 3-inch radial circle according to graphs (page 35), cutting away gray areas.
2. Stitch and Overcast frame and petals following graphs, leaving straight edge of petals unstitched.

SKILL LEVEL
Beginner

SIZE
6 inches W x 6 inches H (15.2cm x 15.2cm), excluding embellishments

MATERIALS
Each
- 2 (4-inch) Uniek QuickShape plastic canvas radial circles
- 5 (3-inch) Uniek QuickShape plastic canvas circles
- #16 tapestry needle
- Hand-sewing needle

Rainbow
- Uniek Needloft plastic canvas yarn as listed in color key
- Shamrock buttons:
    1 (¾-inch/1.9cm)
    2 (½-inch/1.3cm)
- Orange and green thread

Pastel
- Red Heart Classic medium weight yarn Art. E267 as listed in color key
- Red Heart Super Saver medium weight yarn Art. E300 as listed in color key
- 1 each ½-inch (12mm) ribbon roses: white, pink, yellow, purple, blue
- Off-white thread

Denim
- Red Heart Super Saver medium weight yarn Art. E300 as listed in color key
- TLC Essentials medium weight yarn Art. E514 as listed in color key
- 2⅞ x 1⅝-inch (7.3 x 4.1cm) monarch butterfly appliqué
- Navy and black thread

When background stitching and Overcasting are completed, work carrot Running Stitches.

3. Using photo as a guide through step 5 and using hand-sewing needle and navy thread through step 4, overlap and stitch petals around back of frame.

4. Place photo holder behind petals, centered over bottom half of frame, with straight edge behind opening; Whipstitch in place.

5. Using hand-sewing needle and black thread, tack butterfly to frame and petal.

6. For hanging loop, attach a small length soft navy yarn behind petals. •

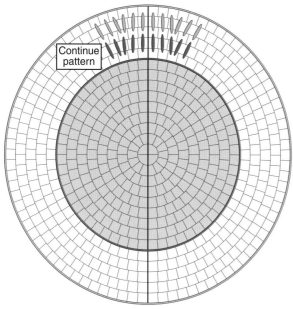

Rainbow Flower Frame
Cut 1 from 4-inch radial circle,
cutting away gray area

COLOR KEY		
RAINBOW FLOWER FRAME		
Yards	**Plastic Canvas Yarn**	
3 (2.8m)	■	Red #01
5 (4.6m)	■	Christmas green #28
5 (4.6m)	■	Royal #32
4 (3.7m)	▨	Bittersweet #52
3 (2.8m)	☐	Yellow #57
5 (4.6m)	╱	Purple #46 Overcast

Color numbers given are for Uniek Needloft plastic canvas yarn.

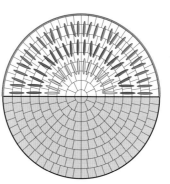

Rainbow Flower Frame Petal
Cut 5 from 3-inch radial circles,
cutting away gray area

COLOR KEY
PASTEL FLOWER FRAME

Yards	Medium Weight Yarn
2 (1.9m)	Cornmeal #320
7 (6.5m)	☐ Baby print #345
2 (1.9m)	Light mint #364
2 (1.9m)	☐ Petal pink #373
2 (1.9m)	Light blue #381
2 (1.9m)	Lavender #584

Color numbers given are for Red Heart Classic medium weight yarn Art. E267 and Super Saver medium weight yarn Art. E300.

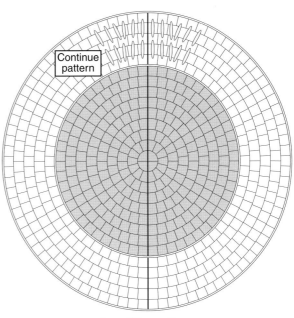

Pastel Flower Frame
Cut 1 from 4-inch radial circle,
cutting away gray area

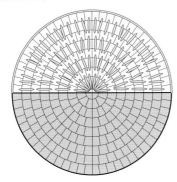

Pastel Flower Frame Petal
Cut 5 from 3-inch radial circles,
cutting away gray area
Stitch 1 as graphed
Stitch 1 each with cornmeal,
light mint, light blue and lavender

COLOR KEY
DENIM FLOWER FRAME

Yards	Medium Weight Yarn
5 (4.6m)	☐ Pumpkin #254
6 (5.5m)	■ Carrot #256
11 (10.1m)	☐ Shaded denim #2968
6 (5.5m)	✐ Soft navy #387 Overcast
	✐ Carrot #256 Running Stitch

Color numbers given are for Red Heart Super Saver medium weight yarn Art. E300 and TLC Essentials medium weight yarn Art. E514.

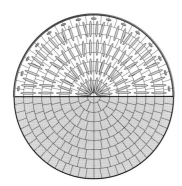

Denim Flower Frame Petal
Cut 5 from 3-inch radial circles,
cutting away gray area

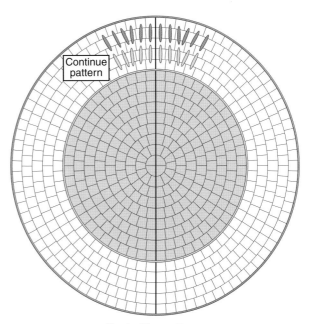

Denim Flower Frame
Cut 1 from 4-inch radial circle,
cutting away gray area

Sunny Quilt Tissue Topper

Bright and cheery, even on a cloudy day, this tissue topper is warm and inviting.

Design by Kathy Wirth

INSTRUCTIONS

1. Cut and stitch plastic canvas according to graphs (this page and page 56).

2. Overcast inside edges on top with light periwinkle. Using white throughout, Whipstitch sides together, then Whipstitch sides to top. Overcast bottom edges. •

GRAPHS CONTINUED ON PAGE 56

Beginner

SIZE

Fits boutique-style tissue box

MATERIALS

- 2 sheets stiff 7-count plastic canvas
- Red Heart Classic medium weight yarn Art. E267 as listed in color key
- Red Heart Kids medium weight yarn Art. E711 as listed in color key
- #16 tapestry needle

Sunny Quilt Tissue Topper Side
31 holes x 37 holes
Cut 4

COLOR KEY

Yards	Medium Weight Yarn
29 (26.6m)	☐ White #1
16 (14.7m)	☐ Light periwinkle #827
23 (21.1m)	■ Olympic blue #849
11 (10.1m)	☐ Yellow #2230
	● Olympic blue #849 French Knot

Color numbers given are for Red Heart Classic medium weight yarn Art. E267 and Kids medium weight yarn Art. E711.

Princess Purse Pack

Delight your favorite fashionable little girl with this tiny tissue pack that mimics a purse.

Design by Deborah Scheblein

INSTRUCTIONS

1. Cut and stitch plastic canvas according to graphs (pages 40 and 41).

2. Using yellow yarn throughout, Whipstitch front and back to sides, then Whipstitch front, back and sides to base. Whipstitch top to back and to flap. Overcast all remaining edges.

3. Using yellow yarn, attach button to front of flap where indicated on graph.

4. For handle, knot one end of ribbon. Thread other end from inside to outside through bottom hole indicated on one side. Pull through to knot. Then thread from outside to inside through top hole indicated on same side.

5. Thread other end of ribbon from inside to outside through top hole on other side piece, then from outside to inside at bottom hole. Knot on the inside at desired length. Trim ends.

6. Glue hook side of hook-and-loop circle to underside of flap behind button. Glue loop side of circle to center front where indicated on graph. •

SKILL LEVEL
Beginner

SIZE
Fits tissue pocket pack

MATERIALS
- 1 sheet 7-count plastic canvas
- Medium weight yarn as listed in color key
- #16 tapestry needle
- 1-inch (2.5cm) button in color desired
- 1 yard (1m) ⅜-inch/9mm-wide yellow satin ribbon
- ¾-inch (1.9cm) hook-and-loop circle
- Glue

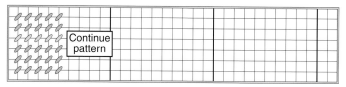

**Princess Purse Pack
Top & Base**
32 holes x 7 holes
Cut 2
Stitch top as graphed
Stitch base entirely with
pink Continental Stitches

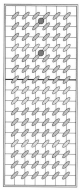

Princess Purse Pack Side
7 holes x 17 holes
Cut 2

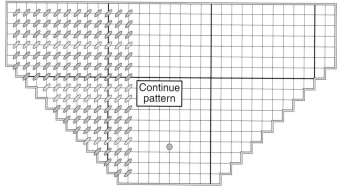

Princess Purse Pack Flap
32 holes x 17 holes
Cut 1

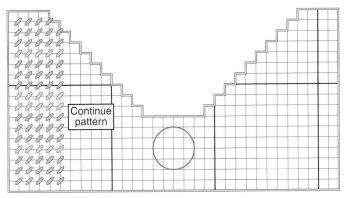

Princess Purse Pack Front
32 holes x 17 holes
Cut 1

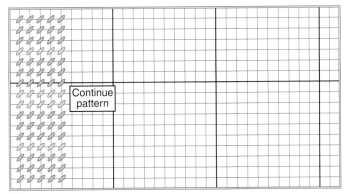

Princess Purse Pack Back
32 holes x 17 holes
Cut 1

COLOR KEY	
Yards	**Medium Weight Yarn**
24 (22m)	▨ Pink
9 (8.3m)	☐ Yellow
	● Attach button
	● Attach ribbon handle
	○ Attach hook-and-loop circle

Camouflage Tissue Holder

SKILL LEVEL
Beginner

SIZE
Fits tissue pocket pack

MATERIALS
- 1 sheet 7-count plastic canvas
- Medium weight yarn as listed in color key
- #16 tapestry needle
- ¾-inch (1.9cm) hook-and-loop circle
- Glue

Add a little fun to a young boy's backpack with this camouflage tissue holder that fits a pocket pack of tissues.

Design by Deborah Scheblein

INSTRUCTIONS

1. Cut plastic canvas according to graphs (pages 43 and 44).
2. Stitch pieces following graphs, working uncoded areas with light brown Continental Stitches.
3. Using medium copper through step 4, tack short edges of handle to back where indicated with blue lines.
4. Whipstitch front and back to sides, then Whipstitch front, back and sides to base. Whipstitch top to back and to flap. Overcast all remaining edges.
5. Glue hook side of hook-and-loop circle to underside of flap and loop side of circle to center front where indicated on graphs. •

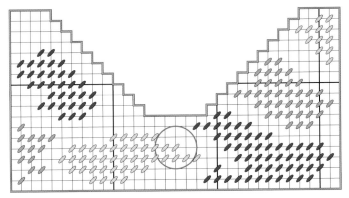

Camouflage Tissue Holder Front
32 holes x 17 holes
Cut 1

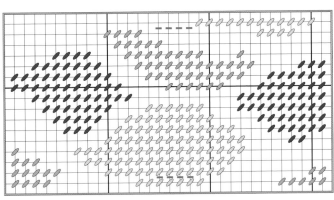

Camouflage Tissue Holder Back
32 holes x 17 holes
Cut 1

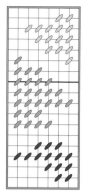

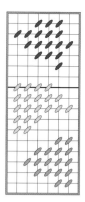

**Camouflage Tissue Holder
Side A**
7 holes x 17 holes
Cut 1

**Camouflage Tissue Holder
Side B**
7 holes x 17 holes
Cut 1

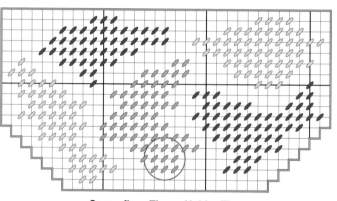

Camouflage Tissue Holder Flap
32 holes x 17 holes
Cut 1

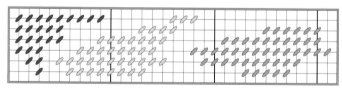

**Camouflage Tissue Holder
Top & Base**
32 holes x 7 holes
Cut 2

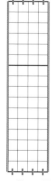

**Camouflage Tissue
Holder Handle**
4 holes x 16 holes
Cut 1

COLOR KEY	
Yards	**Plastic Canvas Yarn**
12 (11m)	▨ Medium copper
7 (6.5m)	▨ Medium green
7 (6.5m)	■ Dark green
13 (11.9m)	Uncoded areas are light brown Continental Stitches
	❘ Attach handle
	○ Attach hook-and-loop circle

Deck of Cards Coasters

Deal up a bit of fun when you serve drinks on this coaster set embellished with the suits of cards.

Design by Angie Arickx

INSTRUCTIONS

1. Cut plastic canvas according to graphs (page 46). Cut one 28-hole x 28-hole piece for tray base. Base will remain unstitched.

2. Stitch coasters and tray sides following graphs, working uncoded areas with white Continental Stitches.

3. Using white throughout, Overcast coasters. Whipstitch tray sides together, then Whipstitch sides to base. Overcast top edges. •

SKILL LEVEL
Beginner

SIZES
Coasters: 4 inches square (10.2cm)

Coaster Tray: 1 inch H x 4⅜ inches square (2.5cm x 11.1cm)

MATERIALS
Each
- 1 sheet 7-count plastic canvas
- Red Heart Super Saver medium weight yarn Art. E300 as listed in color key
- #16 tapestry needle

45

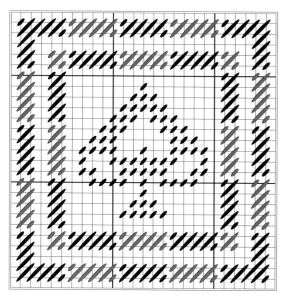

Deck of Cards Coasters
Club Suit Coaster
26 holes x 26 holes
Cut 1

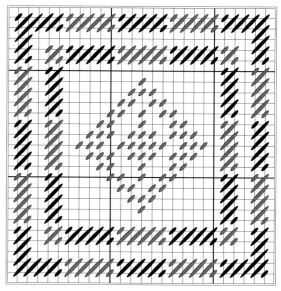

Deck of Cards Coasters
Diamond Suit Coaster
26 holes x 26 holes
Cut 1

46

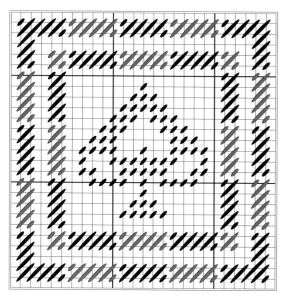

Deck of Cards Coasters
Spade Suit Coaster
26 holes x 26 holes
Cut 1

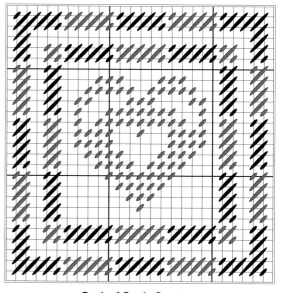

Deck of Cards Coasters
Heart Suit Coaster
26 holes x 26 holes
Cut 1

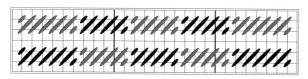

Deck of Cards Coasters
Tray Side
28 holes x 6 holes
Cut 4

COLOR KEY	
Yards	**Medium Weight Yarn**
16 (14.7m)	■ Black #312
14 (12.9m)	▨ Hot red #390
22 (20.2m)	Uncoded areas are white #311 Continental Stitches
	⁄ White #311 Overcast and Whipstitch

Color numbers given are for Red Heart Super Saver medium weight yarn Art. E300.

Pretty in Pink Box

This pretty keepsake box is stitched with regular and iridescent yarn for a sparkly touch that adds beauty.

Design by Betty Hansen

INSTRUCTIONS

1. Cut box sides, lid top and lid sides from clear plastic canvas according to graphs (page 57).

2. From pink plastic canvas, cut one 31 x 31-hole piece for box base, five 29-hole x 29-hole pieces for box liner sides and base, and one 33-hole x 33-hole piece for lid liner. Pink plastic canvas will remain unstitched.

3. Stitch clear pieces following graphs, using a double strand of pink pompadour yarn and one strand pink iridescent craft cord.

4. When background stitching is completed, use pink iridescent craft cord to work Running Stitches on box sides and lid top, and Straight Stitches on lid sides.

5. For handle, thread ends of a length of craft cord from front to back through holes indicated on lid top. Make loop about 1½ inches (3.8cm) long, fastening tails on back side.

6. Using double strand pink pompadour yarn through step 7, Whipstitch box sides together, then Whipstitch sides to unstitched box base. Whipstitch liner sides together, then Whipstitch sides to liner base. Slip liner inside box, then Whipstitch top edges of box and liner together.

CONTINUED ON PAGE 57

SKILL LEVEL
Beginner

SIZE
5⅛ inches W x 5 inches H x 5⅛ inches D (13cm x 12.7cm x 13cm)

MATERIALS
- 2 sheets clear 7-count plastic canvas
- 2 sheets pink 7-count plastic canvas
- Light weight baby yarn as listed in color key
- Uniek Needloft iridescent craft cord as listed in color key
- #16 tapestry needle

Peeper Keepers

Perfect for storing your eyeglasses, these stylish boxes also work nicely to hold lipstick, car keys, credit cards or other tiny items.

Designs by Mary T. Cosgrove

INSTRUCTIONS

1. Cut plastic canvas according to graphs (this page and pages 49 and 50). Cut shocking pink felt slightly smaller than each horizontal keeper piece, and yellow felt slightly smaller than each vertical keeper piece.

2. Stitch pieces following graphs. When background stitching is completed, work parakeet Running Stitches and grenadine and yellow Backstitches.

3. Glue felt to corresponding keeper pieces, making sure there is room for Overcasting and Whipstitching.

4. For each keeper, Whipstitch front and back to sides, then Whipstitch front, back and sides to base. Overcast top edges.

5. For each keeper, cut wire in two 6-inch (15.25cm) lengths. On horizontal front, thread one end through one hole indicated for attaching handle. Twist end of wire around wire above top of canvas to secure.

6. Thread on one bicone bead and six bead chips. Repeat two more times, then end with a fourth bicone bead. Thread wire through remaining hole indicated, twist end of wire around wire above top of canvas.

7. Repeat steps 5 and 6 for horizontal keeper back and for vertical keeper front and back. •

SKILL LEVEL
Beginner

SIZES
Horizontal Keeper:
6⅛ inches W x 3⅛ inches H x 1½ inches D (15.6cm x 8cm x 3.8cm)

Vertical Keeper: 3⅛ inches W x 6⅛ inches H x 1½ inches D (8cm x 15.6cm x 3.8cm)

MATERIALS
Each
- ½ sheet 7-count plastic canvas
- Red Heart Classic medium weight yarn Art. E267 as listed in color key
- Red Heart Kids medium weight yarn Art. E711 as listed in color key
- #16 tapestry needle
- 12 inches (30.5cm) 24-gauge blue craft wire
- 36 turquoise bead chips
- 8 (10mm) rose pink or pink/orange faceted bicone beads
- Hot-glue gun

Horizontal
- 1 sheet shocking pink stiffened Eazy Felt from CPE

Vertical
- 1 sheet yellow stiffened Eazy Felt from CPE

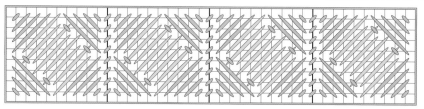

Horizontal Peeper Keeper Base
40 holes x 9 holes
Cut 1

48

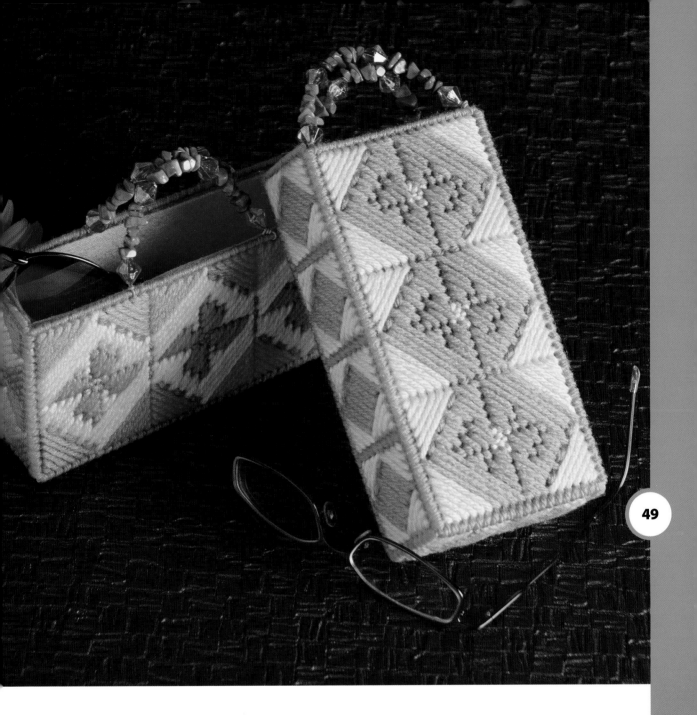

COLOR KEY

Yards	Medium Weight Yarn
22 (20.2m)	▨ Parakeet #513
25 (22.9m)	▨ Grenadine #730
25 (22.9m)	☐ Yellow #2230
	⁄ Parakeet #513 Running Stitch
	⁄ Grenadine #730 Backstitch
	⁄ Yellow #2230 Backstitch
	◎ Attach handle

Color numbers given are for Red Heart Classic worsted weight yarn Art. E267 and Kids medium weight yarn Art. E711.

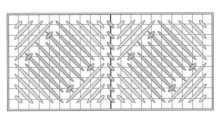

Vertical Peeper Keeper Base
20 holes x 9 holes
Cut 1

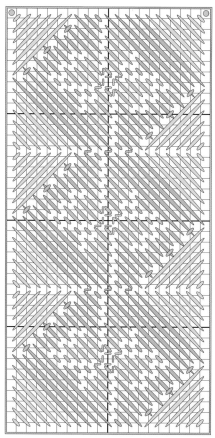

Vertical Peeper Keeper Front & Back
20 holes x 40 holes
Cut 2

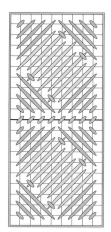

Horizontal Peeper Keeper Side
9 holes x 20 holes
Cut 2

COLOR KEY

Yards	Medium Weight Yarn
22 (20.2m)	☐ Parakeet #513
25 (22.9m)	☐ Grenadine #730
25 (22.9m)	☐ Yellow #2230
	╱ Parakeet #513 Running Stitch
	╱ Grenadine #730 Backstitch
	╱ Yellow #2230 Backstitch
	● Attach handle

Color numbers given are for Red Heart Classic worsted weight yarn Art. E267 and Kids medium weight yarn Art. E711.

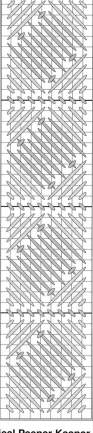

Vertical Peeper Keeper Side
9 holes x 40 holes
Cut 2

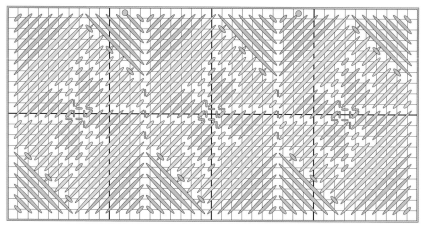

Horizontal Peeper Keeper Front & Back
40 holes x 20 holes
Cut 2

A Gentle Reminder

When life has you scrambling, take a time out and enjoy the humor in this lighthearted message.

Design by Betty Hansen

SKILL LEVEL
Beginner

SIZE
12 inches W x 4⅞ inches H (30.5cm x 12.4cm)

MATERIALS
- ½ sheet clear 7-count plastic canvas
- ½ sheet white 7-count plastic canvas
- Red Heart Classic medium weight yarn Art. 267 as listed in color key
- #16 tapestry needle
- ¾–1-inch (1.9–2.5cm) plastic ring

INSTRUCTIONS

1. Cut one wall hanging from clear plastic canvas for front and one from white plastic canvas for back according to graph (page 52). Back will remain unstitched.

2. Stitch front following graph, working border first. Stitch letters next. Fill in uncoded area with sea coral Continental Stitches.

3. When background stitching is completed, work copper Straight Stitches in holes indicated. **Note:** *Straight Stitches are not worked over intersections, but each is worked in one hole.*

4. Using yarn, attach bottom of ring to center of back so that top of ring is just below top edge.

5. Whipstitch wrong sides of front and back together with bronze. •

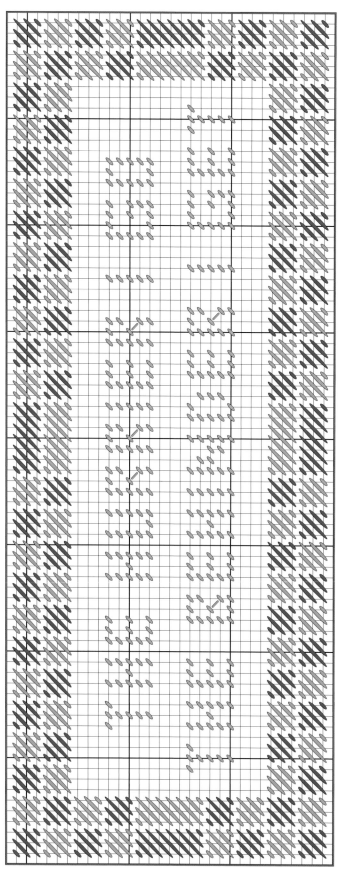

A Gentle Reminder Front & Back
80 holes x 32 holes
Cut 1 from clear for front
Stitch as graphed
Cut 1 from white for back
Do not stitch

COLOR KEY

Yards	Medium Weight Yarn
16 (14.7m)	■ Bronze #286
16 (14.7m)	▨ Copper #289
14 (12.9m)	Uncoded background is sea coral #246 Continental Stitches
	╱ Copper #289 Straight Stitch

Color numbers given are for Red Heart Classic medium weight yarn Art. E267.

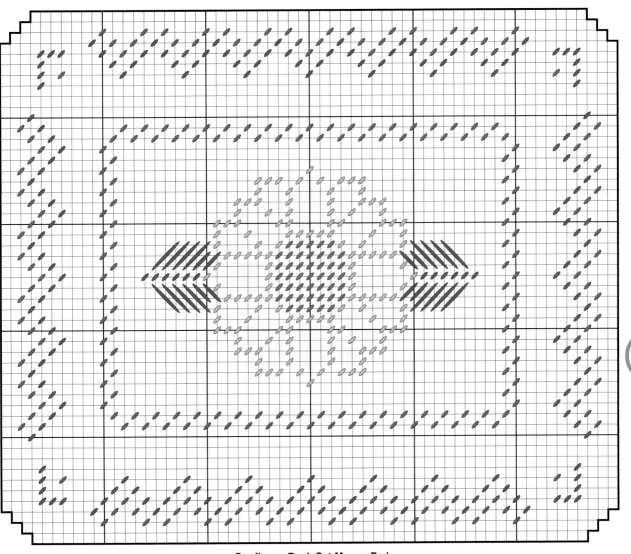

Sunflower Desk Set Mouse Pad
60 holes x 50 holes
Cut 1

COLOR KEY	
Yards	**Medium Weight Yarn**
5 (4.6m)	■ Red
4 (3.7m)	■ Green
4 (3.7m)	■ Gold
2 (1.9m)	■ Dark brown
26 (23.8m)	Uncoded areas on white background are black Continental Stitches
4 (3.7m)	Uncoded areas on yellow background are yellow Continental Stitches
✏ Black Overcast	

Blue Skies Frame

CONTINUED FROM PAGE 22

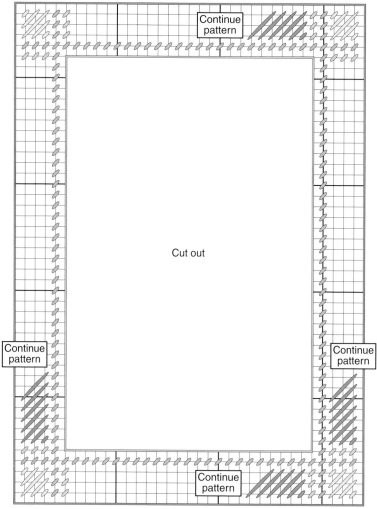

Blue Skies Frame
34 holes x 47 holes
Cut 1

COLOR KEY	
Yards	**Medium Weight Yarn**
7 (6.5m)	■ Cornflower blue
3 (2.8m)	■ Light aqua
2 (1.9m)	□ Orchid
1 (1m)	□ Light blue
1 (1m)	□ Light yellow
1 (1m)	□ Spring green
2 (1.9m)	╱ White Overcast
1 (1m)	╱ Pink Overcast
	○ White French Knot

54

Beach Umbrellas Frame

CONTINUED FROM PAGE 24

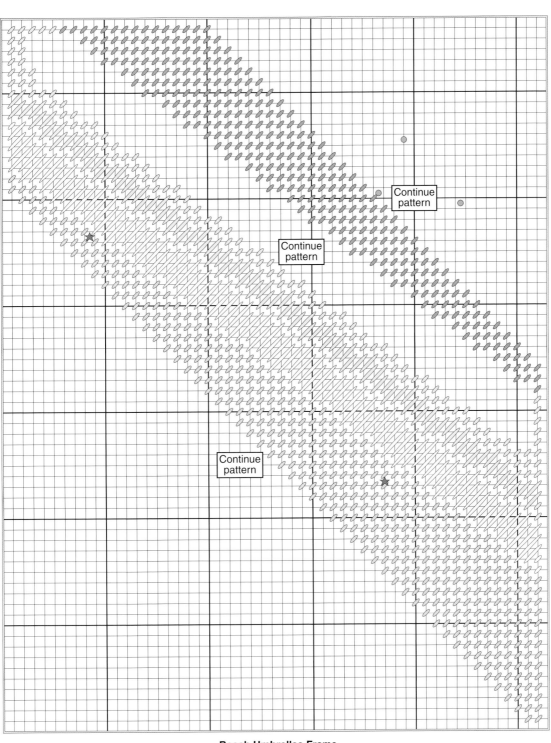

Continue pattern

Continue pattern

Continue pattern

Beach Umbrellas Frame
Beach Scene
53 holes x 67 holes
Cut 1

Sunny Quilt Tissue Topper

CONTINUED FROM PAGE 36

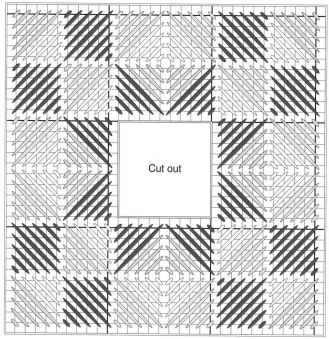

Sunny Quilt Tissue Topper Top
31 holes x 31 holes
Cut 1

COLOR KEY	
Yards	**Medium Weight Yarn**
29 (26.6m)	☐ White #1
16 (14.7m)	☐ Light periwinkle #827
23 (21.1m)	■ Olympic blue #849
11 (10.1m)	☐ Yellow #2230
	● Olympic blue #849 French Knot

Color numbers given are for Red Heart Classic medium weight yarn Art. E267 and Kids medium weight yarn Art. E711.

Pretty in Pink Box

CONTINUED FROM PAGE 47

7. Whipstitch lid sides together. Place liner for lid on wrong side of lid top, then Whipstitch sides to top and liner, working through all three layers. Overcast bottom edges of lid sides. •

Pretty in Pink Box Lid Top
33 holes x 33 holes
Cut 1 from clear

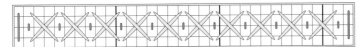

Pretty in Pink Box Lid Side
33 holes x 4 holes
Cut 4 from clear

COLOR KEY

Yards	Light Weight Baby Yarn
95 (86.9m)	☐ Pink pompadour (2 strands)
	Iridescent Craft Cord
25 (22.9m)	▨ Pink #55050
	╱ Pink #55050 Straight Stitch and Running Stitch
	● Attach pink #55050 handle

Color number given is for Uniek Needloft iridescent craft cord.

Pretty in Pink Box Side
31 holes x 31 holes
Cut 4 from clear

Designs to Make in a Day

Quick and easy to create,
each project in this
collection of designs
is easily created in
a day or less.

Chicken Napkin Holder

Keep napkins close at hand with this darling holder featuring brightly colored chickens.

Design by Gina Woods

SKILL LEVEL
Beginner

SIZE
7 inches W x 3½ inches H x 2 inches D (17.8cm x 8.9cm x 5.1cm)

MATERIALS
- 1 sheet 7-count plastic canvas
- Small amount colored 7-count plastic canvas to match or complement holder
- Medium weight yarn as listed in color key
- #16 tapestry needle
- 2 (4mm) round black beads
- Hand-sewing needle and black thread
- Hot-glue gun

INSTRUCTIONS

1. Cut plastic canvas according to graphs. Cut one 46-hole x 13-hole piece for base from colored canvas to match or complement holder. Base will remain unstitched.

2. Stitch and Overcast one chicken as graphed, working uncoded area with bright yellow Continental Stitches. Reverse remaining chicken before stitching and Overcasting.

3. For eyes, use hand-sewing needle and black thread to attach beads to chickens where indicated on graph.

4. Stitch holder front, back and ends in desired colored (sample used navy blue). Whipstitch front and back to ends, then Whipstitch front, back and ends to unstitched base. Overcast top edges.

5. Using photo as a guide, glue chickens to holder front. •

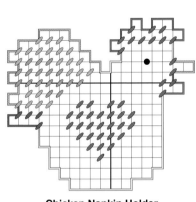

**Chicken Napkin Holder
Chicken**
18 holes x 16 holes
Cut 2, reverse 1

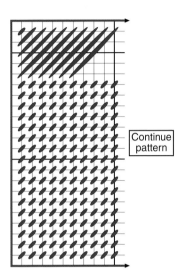

Continue pattern

**Chicken Napkin Holder
Front & Back**
46 holes x 23 holes
Cut 2

**Chicken Napkin Holder
End**
13 holes x 23 holes
Cut 2

COLOR KEY	
Yards	**Medium Weight Yarn**
38 (34.8m)	■ Holder color as desired
3 (2.8m)	■ Red
2 (1.9m)	▨ Red-violet
1 (1m)	■ Green
1 (1m)	▨ Blue
4 (3.7m)	Uncoded area on chicken is bright yellow Continental Stitches
	⁄ Bright yellow Overcast
1 (1m)	⁄ Yellow-orange Overcast
	● Attach bead

Chicken Towel Holder

Display a decorative towel in style when you drape it from this cheeky chicken.

Design by Debra Arch

INSTRUCTIONS

1. Cut body, comb and beak pieces from stiff plastic canvas; cut tail from black plastic canvas according to graphs (page 64).

2. Following graphs throughout, stitch and Overcast beak and tail. Stitch body and comb pieces, using two strands white when stitching body.

3. When background stitching is completed, work black braid Straight Stitches on body pieces.

4. Place upper half of ring between body pieces as in photo. Whipstitch body pieces together, working around ring at bottom edge.

5. Make several ¾-inch (1.9cm) loops with white yarn at center top edge of body.

6. Overcast bottom edges of combs, then Whipstitch combs together along remaining edges. Slip comb over top of head, pushing loops down in front; glue in place.

7. Glue beak to body front where indicated with yellow lines. For eyes, glue cabochons to body where indicated on graph. Glue tail to body back as in photo.

8. Use cotton swab to apply blush to cheek areas. •

SKILL LEVEL
Beginner

SIZE
4⅝ inches W x 8⅛ inches H (11.7cm x 20.6cm), including ring

MATERIALS
- ½ sheet clear stiff 7-count plastic canvas
- ¼ sheet black 7-count plastic canvas
- Red Heart Super Saver medium weight yarn Art. E300 as listed in color key
- Red Heart Plush medium weight yarn Art. E719 as listed in color key
- Uniek Needloft plastic canvas yarn as listed in color key
- Kreinik Heavy (#32) Braid as listed in color key
- #16 tapestry needle
- 2 (6mm) black cabochons
- 3-inch gold metal ring
- Red blush and cotton swab
- Hot-glue gun

62

Chicken Towel Holder Tail
25 holes x 23 holes
Cut 1 from black

**Chicken Towel Holder
Comb**
9 holes x 8 holes
Cut 2 from stiff

**Chicken Towel Holder
Beak**
7 holes x 5 holes
Cut 1 from stiff

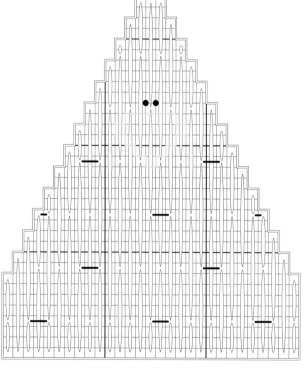

Chicken Towel Holder Body
29 holes x 34 holes
Cut 2 from stiff

COLOR KEY		
Yards	**Medium Weight Yarn**	
4 (3.7m)	■ Hot red #390	
30 (27.5m)	□ White #9001 (2 strands)	
	╱ Hot red #390 Straight Stitch	
	Plastic Canvas Yarn	
1 (1m)	▨ Yellow #57	
	Heavy (#32) Braid	
8 (7.4m)	■ Black #005	
	╱ Black #005 Straight Stitch	
	● Attach black cabochon	

Color numbers given are for Red Heart Super Saver medium weight yarn Art. E300 and Plush medium weight yarn Art. E719, Uniek Needloft plastic canvas yarn and Kreinik Heavy (#32) Braid.

Chicken Recipe-Card Holder

Your favorite recipe will be right at home held in the tail feathers or under the beak of this darling chicken recipe keeper.

Design by Debra Arch

SKILL LEVEL
Beginner

SIZE
5½ inches W x 6¾ inches H (14cm x 17.1cm)

MATERIALS
- ½ sheet clear stiff 7-count plastic canvas
- ¼ sheet black 7-count plastic canvas
- Red Heart Super Saver medium weight yarn Art. E300 as listed in color key
- Red Heart Plush medium weight yarn Art. E719 as listed in color key
- Uniek Needloft plastic canvas yarn as listed in color key
- Kreinik Heavy (#32) Braid as listed in color key
- #16 tapestry needle
- 2 (6mm) black cabochons
- ½ cup clear marbles
- Red blush and cotton swab
- Hot-glue gun

65

INSTRUCTIONS

1. Cut body, base, comb and beak pieces from stiff plastic canvas; cut tails from black plastic canvas according to graphs. Base will remain unstitched.

2. Following graphs throughout, stitch and Overcast beak. Stitch body, tail and comb pieces, using two strands when stitching with white.

3. When background stitching is completed, use black braid to work Straight Stitches on body pieces and Backstitches on single tail.

4. Whipstitch body pieces together around side and top edges. Whipstitch base to sides, adding marbles before closing.

5. Make several ¾-inch (1.9cm) loops with white yarn at center top edge of body.

6. Overcast bottom edges of combs, then Whipstitch combs together along remaining edges. Slip comb over top of head, pushing loops down in front; glue in place.

7. Overcast single tail and around side and top edges of double tail from dot to dot. Fold double tail

in half, insert single tail inside fold and Whipstitch together along remaining edges.

8. Glue beak to body front where indicated with yellow lines. For eyes, glue cabochons to body where indicated on graph. Center and glue tail to body back where desired.

9. Use cotton swab to apply blush to cheek areas. •

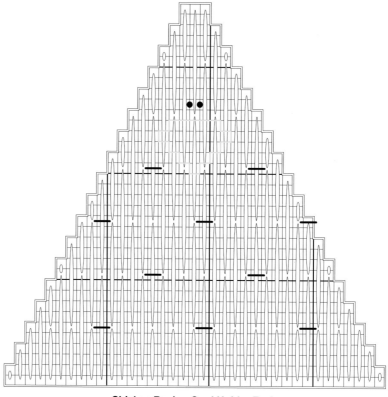

Chicken Recipe-Card Holder Body
37 holes x 36 holes
Cut 2 from stiff

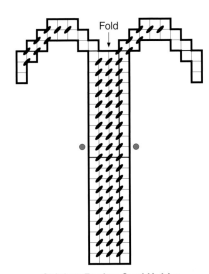

**Chicken Recipe-Card Holder
Double Tail**
18 holes x 23 holes
Cut 1 from black

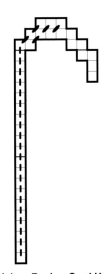

**Chicken Recipe-Card Holder
Single Tail**
8 holes x 23 holes
Cut 1 from black

**Chicken Recipe-Card Holder
Comb**
9 holes x 8 holes
Cut 2 from stiff

**Chicken Recipe-Card Holder
Beak**
7 holes x 5 holes
Cut 1 from stiff

67

COLOR KEY

Yards	Medium Weight Yarn
4 (3.7m)	■ Hot red #390
36 (33m)	☐ White #9001 (2 strands)
	╱ Hot red #390 Straight Stitch
	Plastic Canvas Yarn
1 (1m)	☐ Yellow #57
	Heavy (#32) Braid
10 (9.2m)	■ Black #005
	╱ Black #005 Straight Stitch
	● Attach black cabochon

Color numbers given are for Red Heart Super
Saver medium weight yarn Art. E300 and Plush
medium weight yarn Art. E719, Uniek Needloft
plastic canvas yarn and Kreinik Heavy (#32)
Braid.

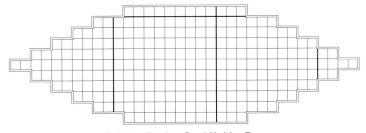

Chicken Recipe-Card Holder Base
34 holes x 11 holes
Cut 1 from stiff
Do not stitch

Tiny Frames Trio

You'll want to stitch several of these and display your child's school photo at home and at the office!

Designs by Nancy Dorman

INSTRUCTIONS

1. Cut plastic canvas according to graphs (this page and page 95). Cut felt slightly smaller all around than each frame. Do not cut out photo openings in felt.

2. Stitch and Overcast pieces following graphs, working floss embroidery when Background stitching and Overcasting are completed.

3. Cut magnet into three equal lengths. Cut ribbon into two equal lengths; tie each in a bow, trimming tails as desired.

4. Cut photos to fit frames, then center and glue behind openings. Glue felt behind photos; glue magnets to center top of felt.

5. Using photo as guide, glue one bow to center bottom of heart frame and one to upper left corner of oval frame.

6. Place heavy book or weighted object on frames until dry. •

GRAPHS CONTINUED ON PAGE 95

SKILL LEVEL
Beginner

SIZES
Heart Frame: 3¼ inches W x 3¼ inches H (8.3cm x 8.3cm)

Oval Frame: 2⅝ inches W x 3⅜ inches H (6.7cm x 8.6cm)

Rectangle Frame: 2⅝ inches W x 3¾ inches H (6.7cm x 9.5cm)

MATERIALS
- ½ sheet 7-count plastic canvas
- Medium weight yarn as listed in color key
- 6-strand embroidery floss as listed in color key
- #16 tapestry needle
- ½ sheet white felt
- 18 inches (45.7cm) ⅛-inch/3mm-wide white ribbon
- 3 inches (7.6cm) magnet strip
- Heavy book or weighted object
- Craft glue

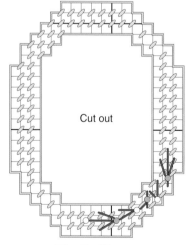

Tiny Oval Frame
17 holes x 22 holes
Cut 1

COLOR KEY	
Yards	**Medium Weight Yarn**
5 (4.6m)	☐ Light rose
5 (4.6m)	☐ Light green
5 (4.6m)	☐ Ivory
	6-Strand Embroidery Floss
2 (1.9m)	╱ Green Backstitch and Straight Stitch
1 (1m)	○ White French Knot
1 (1m)	● Light rose French Knot

Cut out

Bluebird & Robin Sit-Arounds

Bird lovers will delight in decorating with a tiny bluebird and robin.

Designs by Robin Petrina

INSTRUCTIONS

1. Cut plastic canvas according to graphs (pages 71 and 72), carefully cutting apart each bird at corners where indicated with green lines.
2. Following graphs throughout, Overcast beaks. Stitch and Overcast wings, stitching one wing for bluebird as graphed.

Reverse remaining wing and work stitches in reverse. Repeat for robin, replacing delft blue with mid brown.
3. Stitch and Overcast one tail as graphed for bluebird. Stitch and Overcast remaining tail for robin, replacing delft blue with mid brown.

SKILL LEVEL
Intermediate

SIZES
2⅝ inches W x 3½ inches H x 4 inches D (6.7cm x 8.9cm x 10.2cm)

MATERIALS
Each
- ¾ sheet 7-count plastic canvas
- Red Heart Super Saver medium weight yarn Art. E300 as listed in color key
- #16 tapestry needle
- Polyester fiberfill
- Hot-glue gun
Robin
- Red Heart Classic medium weight yarn Art. E267 as listed in color key

4. Stitch bird bodies, working French Knots for eyes when background stitching is completed.
5. For each bird, Whipstitch body sections together, easing as necessary to fit and stuffing with polyester fiberfill before closing last section. Whipstitch top edges of head together, matching colored brackets.
6. Using photo as a guide, for each bird, glue wrong sides of two beak pieces together, then glue beak at brackets to head. Glue wings to body sides and tail to body back where indicated with red line. •

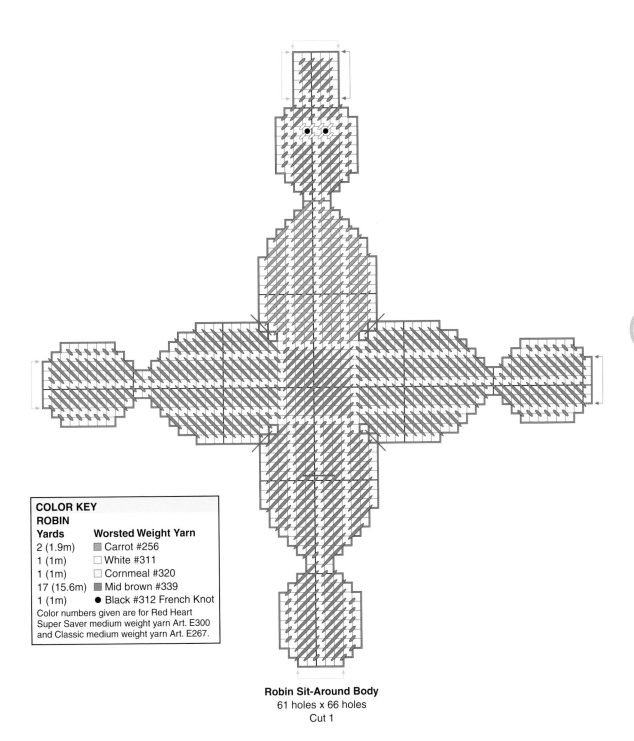

COLOR KEY
ROBIN

Yards	Worsted Weight Yarn
2 (1.9m)	▨ Carrot #256
1 (1m)	☐ White #311
1 (1m)	☐ Cornmeal #320
17 (15.6m)	▥ Mid brown #339
1 (1m)	● Black #312 French Knot

Color numbers given are for Red Heart Super Saver medium weight yarn Art. E300 and Classic medium weight yarn Art. E267.

Robin Sit-Around Body
61 holes x 66 holes
Cut 1

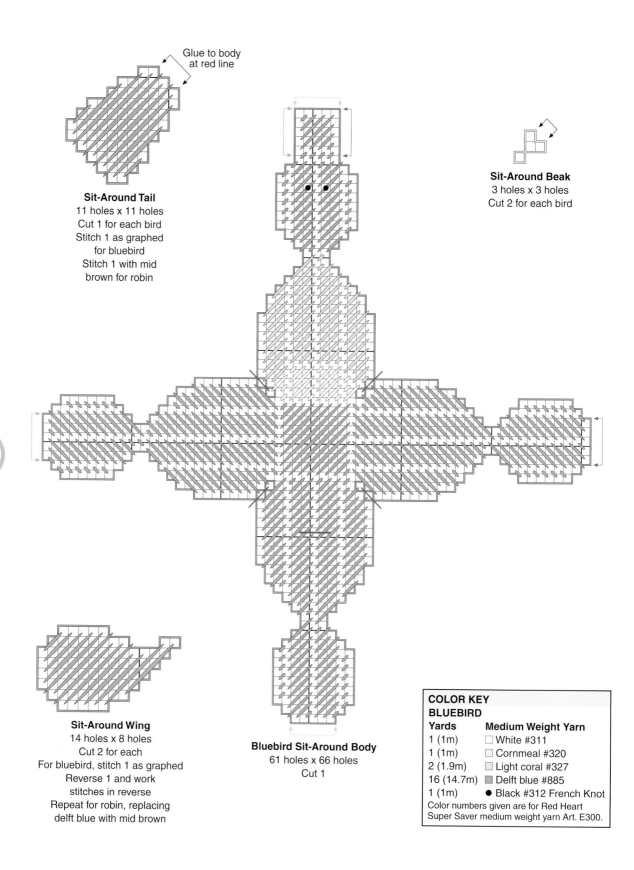

Glue to body
at red line

Sit-Around Tail
11 holes x 11 holes
Cut 1 for each bird
Stitch 1 as graphed
for bluebird
Stitch 1 with mid
brown for robin

Sit-Around Beak
3 holes x 3 holes
Cut 2 for each bird

72

Sit-Around Wing
14 holes x 8 holes
Cut 2 for each
For bluebird, stitch 1 as graphed
Reverse 1 and work
stitches in reverse
Repeat for robin, replacing
delft blue with mid brown

Bluebird Sit-Around Body
61 holes x 66 holes
Cut 1

COLOR KEY
BLUEBIRD

Yards	Medium Weight Yarn
1 (1m)	☐ White #311
1 (1m)	☐ Cornmeal #320
2 (1.9m)	☐ Light coral #327
16 (14.7m)	☐ Delft blue #885
1 (1m)	● Black #312 French Knot

Color numbers given are for Red Heart
Super Saver medium weight yarn Art. E300.

Autumn Leaf Beverage Tags

These leaf-shaped tags are the perfect way for your guests to keep track of their beverages!

Design by Sue Penrod

INSTRUCTIONS

1. Cut plastic canvas according to graph.

2. Stitch pieces following graph, working one with light tangerine as graphed, one with tangerine, one with very dark coffee brown and one with medium copper.

3. Fold leaves in half, matching edges of leaves; Whipstitch together with adjacent colors, leaving edges between arrows unstitched.

4. Open hoop and thread on two light blue beads. Slip end of hoop through fold of light tangerine leaf, then add last two light blue beads. Bend straight end of hoop up at a 90 degree angle and slip through loop on other end.

5. Repeat with remaining leaves,

using green beads with tangerine leaf, red beads with very dark coffee brown leaf and yellow beads with medium copper leaf.

6. Place hoops around stem on stemware, soda pop tab, mug handle, etc., then slip bend on hoop into loop on other end. •

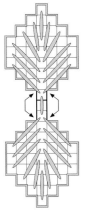

Beverage Tag Leaf
7 holes x 19 holes
Cut 4
Stitch 1 as graphed
Stitch 1 each with tangerine,
very dark coffee brown
and medium copper

COLOR KEY	
Yards	**6-Strand Embroidery Floss**
2 (1.9m)	Tangerine #740
2 (1.9m)	☐ Light tangerine #742
2 (1.9m)	Very dark coffee brown #898
2 (1.9m)	Medium copper #920
Color numbers given are for DMC 6-strand embroidery floss.	

SKILL LEVEL
Beginner

SIZE
1 inch W x ¾ inch H (2.5cm x 1.9cm), excluding hoop

MATERIALS
- Small amount 10-count plastic canvas
- DMC 6-strand embroidery floss as listed in color key
- #18 tapestry needle
- 4 (4mm) beads each: light blue, green, red and yellow
- 4 (1⅛-inch) wine glass ID tag hoops or ear wire hoops

Tropical Fish Tote

Featuring minimal stitching and colored canvas, this simplistic tote will look gorgeous on the beach or as a gift bag.

Design by Terry Ricioli

INSTRUCTIONS

1. Cut front and back from bright green plastic canvas according to graph (page 96).

2. From bright pink plastic canvas, cut one 70-hole x 19-hole piece for base, two 19-hole x 60-hole pieces for sides and two 4-hole x 70-hole pieces for handles. Base, sides and handles will remain unstitched.

3. Stitch front and back following graph.

4. Using pink yarn throughout, Whipstitch front and back to sides, then Whipstitch front, back and sides to base. Overcast top edges. While Overcasting, Whipstitch ends of one handle to front and ends of remaining handle to back where indicated. •

GRAPH ON PAGE 96

74

SKILL LEVEL
Beginner

SIZE
10¾ inches W x 9¼ inches H x 3 inches D (27.3cm x 23.5cm x 7.6cm), excluding handles

MATERIALS
- 2 sheets bright green 7-count plastic canvas
- 1 sheet bright pink 7-count plastic canvas
- Medium weight yarn as listed in color key
- #16 tapestry needle

Tropical Fish Coasters

Swimming in a gentle waves holder, these funky tropical fish coasters will add pizzazz to any meal.

Designs by Terry Ricioli

INSTRUCTIONS

1. Following graphs throughout, cut holder front and back from bright green plastic canvas; cut two each of fish coasters from bright green and bright pink plastic canvas.

2. From bright pink plastic canvas, cut one 32-hole x 12-hole piece for base and two 12-hole x 10-hole pieces for sides. Base and sides will remain unstitched.

3. Stitch front, back and coasters following graphs.

4. Do not Overcast edges of coasters. Using pink yarn, Whipstitch front and back to sides, then Whipstitch front, back and sides to base. Do not Overcast top edges. •

SKILL LEVEL
Beginner

SIZES
Coasters: 4⅝ inches W x 4¼ inches H (11.7cm x 10.8cm)

Coaster Holder: 5 inches W x 2⅛ inches H x 2 inches D (12.7cm x 5.4cm x 5.1cm)

MATERIALS
- 2 sheets bright green 7-count plastic canvas
- 1 sheet bright pink 7-count plastic canvas
- Medium weight yarn as listed in color key
- #16 tapestry needle

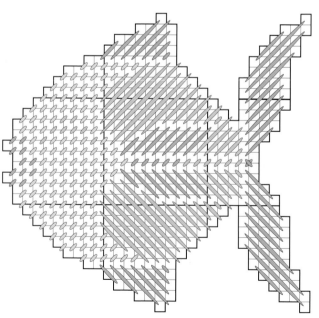

Tropical Fish Coaster
30 holes x 28 holes
Cut 2 from bright green
Cut 2 from bright pink

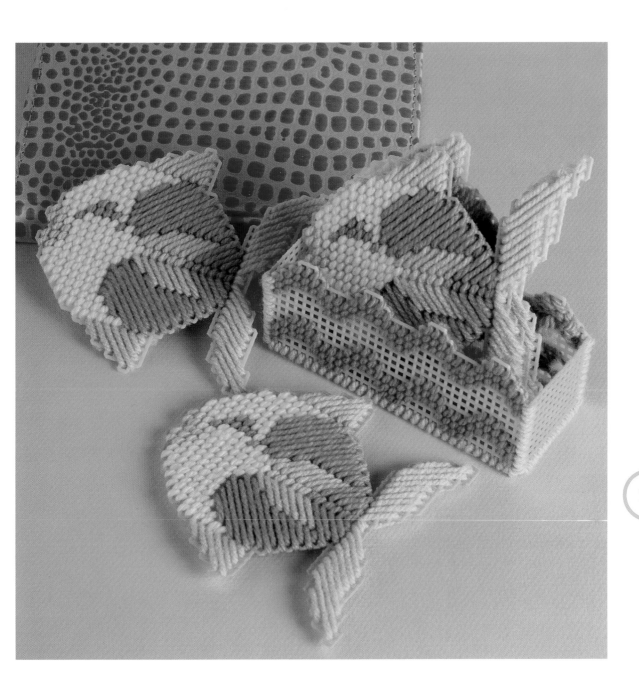

COLOR KEY

Yards	Medium Weight Yarn
16 (14.7m)	☐ Turquoise
12 (11m)	☐ Yellow
10 (9.2m)	☐ Pink

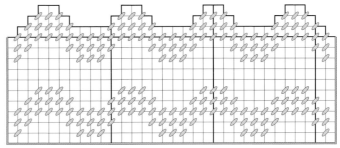

Tropical Fish Coasters Holder
Front & Back
32 holes x 13 holes
Cut 2 from bright green

ID Holders

Ideal for holding a student ID card or a driver's license, these quick-to-stitch pockets make great gifts.

Designs by Debra Arch

PROJECT NOTE

Use 1 strand when stitching with yarn and 2 strands when stitching with ribbon unless otherwise instructed.

INSTRUCTIONS

1. Cut holder fronts from stiff plastic canvas according to graphs (this page and pages 80 and 81). Cut holder backs in colored plastic canvas to coordinate with fronts. Backs will remain unstitched.
2. Stitch monogram front following graph, working purple Slanted Gobelin Stitches first. Choose monogram desired from alphabet (page 81), then center and stitch letter. Fill in background with orchid Continental Stitches.
3. Stitch remaining front pieces following graphs, working Continental Stitches in uncoded areas as follows: angel with lilac, flower with fern and heart flag with sandstone. Use two strands bright blue to stitch angel's gown.
4. When background stitching is completed, work pearl ribbon Straight Stitch for angel's halo and #5 pearl cotton French Knots for angel's eyes.

5. Overcast top edges of front pieces, then Whipstitch fronts to corresponding back pieces. •

SKILL LEVEL
Beginner

SIZES
Quilt Holder: 3 inches W x 3¼ inches H (7.6cm x 8.3cm)

All Remaining Holders: 2⅞ inches W x 3¼ inches H (7.3cm x 8.3cm)

MATERIALS
- 1 sheet clear stiff 7-count plastic canvas
- Small amounts colored 7-count plastic canvas in coordinating colors
- Uniek Needloft plastic canvas yarn as listed in color key
- Kreinik ⅛-inch Ribbon as listed in color key
- #5 pearl cotton as listed in color key
- #16 tapestry needle

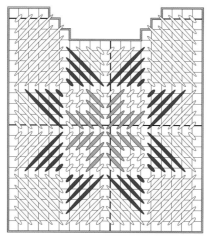

Quilt ID Holder Front & Back
19 holes x 21 holes
Cut 1 from stiff for front
Stitch as graphed
Cut 1 from colored canvas for back
Do not stitch

COLOR KEY		
QUILT		
Yards	**Plastic Canvas Yarn**	
3 (2.8m)	▨ Maple #13	
2 (1.9m)	■ Forest #29	
5 (4.6m)	☐ White #41	
Color numbers given are for Uniek Needloft plastic canvas yarn.		

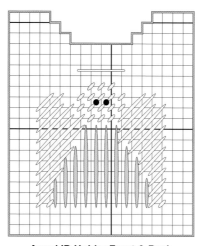

Angel ID Holder Front & Back
18 holes x 21 holes
Cut 1 from stiff for front
Stitch as graphed
Cut 1 from colored canvas for back
Do not stitch

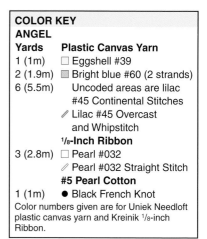

COLOR KEY
ANGEL

Yards	Plastic Canvas Yarn
1 (1m)	☐ Eggshell #39
2 (1.9m)	☐ Bright blue #60 (2 strands)
6 (5.5m)	Uncoded areas are lilac #45 Continental Stitches
	⁄ Lilac #45 Overcast and Whipstitch
¹/₈-Inch Ribbon	
3 (2.8m)	☐ Pearl #032
	⁄ Pearl #032 Straight Stitch
#5 Pearl Cotton	
1 (1m)	● Black French Knot

Color numbers given are for Uniek Needloft plastic canvas yarn and Kreinik ¹/₈-inch Ribbon.

COLOR KEY
FLOWER

Yards	Plastic Canvas Yarn
2 (1.9m)	☐ White #41
1 (1m)	☐ Yellow #57
3 (2.8m)	☐ Bright orange #58
7 (6.5m)	Uncoded areas are fern #23 Continental Stitches
	⁄ Fern #23 Overcast and Whipstitch

Color numbers given are for Uniek Needloft plastic canvas yarn.

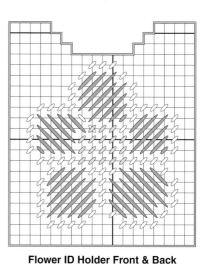

Flower ID Holder Front & Back
18 holes x 21 holes
Cut 1 from stiff for front
Stitch as graphed
Cut 1 from colored canvas for back
Do not stitch

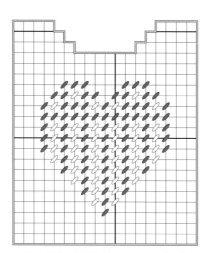

Heart Flag ID Holder Front & Back
18 holes x 21 holes
Cut 1 from stiff for front
Stitch as graphed
Cut 1 from colored canvas for back
Do not stitch

COLOR KEY
HEART FLAG

Yards	Plastic Canvas Yarn
6 (5.5m)	Uncoded areas are sandstone #16 Continental Stitches
	⁄ Sandstone #16 Overcast and Whipstitch
¹/₈-Inch Ribbon	
2 (1.9m)	■ Red #003
2 (1.9m)	■ Sapphire hi lustre #051HL
2 (1.9m)	☐ White #100

Color numbers given are for Uniek Needloft plastic canvas yarn and Kreinik ¹/₈-inch Ribbon.

80

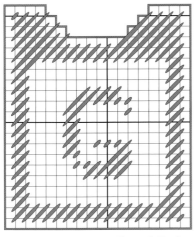

Monogram ID Holder Front & Back
18 holes x 21 holes
Cut 1 from stiff for front
Stitch as graphed
Cut 1 from colored canvas for back
Do not stitch

COLOR KEY
MONOGRAM

Yards	Plastic Canvas Yarn
5 (4.6m)	■ Purple #46
4 (3.7m)	Uncoded areas are orchid #44 Continental Stitches
	╱ Purple #46 Straight Stitch

Color numbers given are for Uniek Needloft plastic canvas yarn.

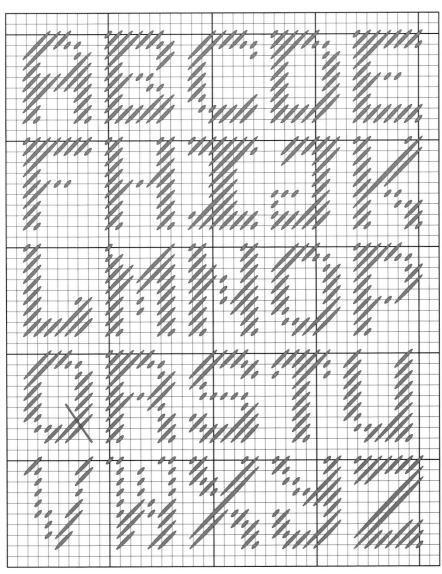

Monogram ID Holder Alphabet

Button Basket Trio

Fill these small baskets with tiny treats for quick and easy gifts or party favors.

Designs by Gina Woods

SKILL LEVEL
Beginner

SIZES
Baskets: 3⅝ inches W x 4⅜ inches H x 2⅜ inches D (9.2cm x 11.1cm x 6cm), including handle

Playful Cat: 2¼ inches W x 2⅜ inches H (5.7cm x 6cm)

Scottie Dog: 3⅛ inches W x 2⅝ inches H (8cm x 6.7cm)

Penguin: 3 inches W x 2⅞ inches H (7.6cm x 7.3cm), including feet

MATERIALS
Each
- ¼ sheet clear 7-count plastic canvas
- Medium weight yarn as listed in color key
- #16 tapestry needle
- Hand-sewing needle and matching thread
- Hot-glue gun

Playful Cat
- Small amount white plastic canvas
- 1½ inches (3.8cm) rose medium weight yarn
- 1 yard (1m) aqua light sport weight yarn
- ½-inch (1.3cm) pink bow button
- 2 novelty buttons of choice (sample used small fish and 1¼-inch/3.2cm fishbowl)

Scottie Dog
- Small amount tan plastic canvas
- 6-strand embroidery floss as listed in color key
- ⅜-inch (1cm) metal charm for dog tag (sample used gold heart)
- 2 novelty buttons of choice (sample used ¾-inch/1.9cm plaid hearts)

Penguin
- Small amount light blue plastic canvas
- 2 (8mm) movable eyes
- Small amount orange craft foam
- 2 novelty buttons of choice (sample used 1-inch/2.5cm snowflakes)

CUTTING & STITCHING

1. For each basket, cut two 23-hole x 15-hole pieces for front and back, two 15-hole x 15-hole pieces for ends and one 4-hole x 40-hole piece for handle from clear plastic canvas.

2. Cut cat, dog and penguin from clear plastic canvas according to graphs (page 97).

3. For each basket base, cut one 23-hole x 15-hole piece from plastic canvas as follows: cat from white, dog from tan and penguin from light blue. Bases will remain unstitched.

4. From orange craft foam, cut one ⅜-inch-wide x ⅜-inch-high (1cm x 1cm) triangle for penguin's beak and two ⅝-inch-wide x ½-inch-high (1.6cm x 1.3cm) triangles for penguin's feet.

5. Work basket fronts, backs, ends and handles with Continental Stitches as follows: cat with white, dog with tan and penguin with light blue.

6. Stitch and Overcast cat, dog and penguin following graphs, working uncoded areas on dog and penguin with black Continental Stitches.

7. When background stitching is completed, work burgundy yarn and kelly green floss Backstitches on dog, working kelly green Backstitches over red Overcast edges on dog's back as indicated.

8. Using adjacent colors throughout, for each basket Overcast handle. Whipstitch front and back to ends, then Whipstitch front, back and ends to unstitched base. Center and glue handle ends inside basket front and back near top edges.

ASSEMBLY

1. Use photo as a guide throughout assembly. Using hand-sewing needle and matching thread, center and sew novelty buttons to corresponding basket ends.

2. For cat's collar, thread pink bow button to center of rose yarn, then wrap around cat's neck where indicated on graph. Secure on back side, trimming ends as needed.

3. Center and glue cat to basket front. Tie one end of aqua yarn in a bow on top of handle. Allow yarn to drape to front of basket; curl in front of cat, then tack in place; trim end.

4. For dog's collar, thread charm to center of a 2-inch (5.1cm) length of burgundy yarn, then wrap around dog's neck. Secure on back side, trimming ends as needed.

5. Center and glue dog to basket front.

6. Glue beak and feet to penguin. Center and glue penguin to basket front. •

GRAPHS ON PAGE 97

Diamonds & Jewels Frame

A girl can never have too many bags and this funky purse frame is no exception. Frame your favorite photo for girly goodness!

Design by Mary Nell Wall

SKILL LEVEL
Beginner

SIZE
7 inches W x 9⅛ inches H (17.8cm x 23.2cm) with 3¾ inch x 2¼-inch (9.5cm x 5.7cm) opening

MATERIALS
- 1 sheet 7-count plastic canvas
- Red Heart Super Saver medium weight yarn Art. E300 as listed in color key
- #16 tapestry needle
- 24 (5mm) light blue acrylic faceted stones
- 4 x 6-inch (10.2cm x 15.2cm) acrylic photo frame
- Craft glue or hot-glue gun

INSTRUCTIONS
1. Cut plastic canvas according to graphs.
2. Stitch pieces following graphs, working uncoded areas with black Continental Stitches.
3. Using turqua and spring green, Overcast all edges with a Striped Overcast, first using one color in every other hole. Using second color, Overcast remaining edges in every other hole.
4. Glue acrylic stones to stitched frame and handle where indicated on graphs.
5. Glue handle ends to top back side of frame where indicated on graph. Center and glue stitched frame over front of acrylic frame. •

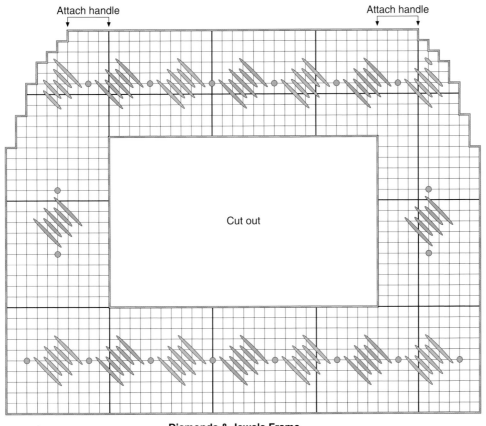

Attach handle   **Attach handle**

Cut out

Diamonds & Jewels Frame
46 holes x 36 holes
Cut 1

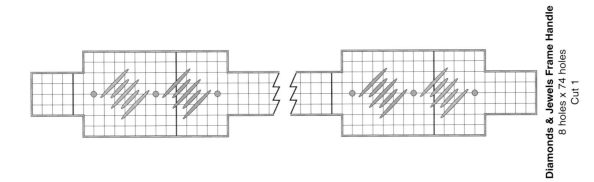

Diamonds & Jewels Frame Handle
8 holes x 74 holes
Cut 1

COLOR KEY

Yards	Medium Weight Yarn
15 (13.8m)	▨ Turqua #512
4 (3.7m)	▢ Spring green #672
16 (14.7m)	Uncoded areas are black #312 Continental Stitches
	● Attach acrylic stone

Color numbers given are for Red Heart Super Saver medium weight yarn Art. E300.

Buttons & Stripes Purse Frame

SKILL LEVEL
Beginner

SIZE
6¼ inches W x 6¼ inches H (15.9cm x 15.9cm) with 3⅝ inch x 2¾-inch (9.2cm x 7cm) opening

MATERIALS
- ½ sheet 7-count plastic canvas
- Red Heart Classic medium weight yarn Art. E267 as listed in color key
- #16 tapestry needle
- 14 (6mm) acrylic faceted stones in assorted colors
- 14 (¼ to ⅜-inch/0.6 to 1cm) buttons in assorted colors
- ⅝-inch (1.6cm) button in desired color
- 5 x 3½-inch (12.7cm x 8.9cm) acrylic photo frame
- Craft glue or hot-glue gun

Stripes created with stitches and brightly colored buttons add a touch of whimsy to this fun frame.

Design by Mary Nell Wall

INSTRUCTIONS
1. Cut plastic canvas according to graphs.

2. Stitch and Overcast pieces following graphs, working white Backstitches when background stitching is completed.

3. Glue handle ends to top front of stitched frame where indicated with red lines.

4. Using photo as a guide, glue 13 smaller buttons to frame and handle ends where indicated on graphs. Glue ⅝-inch (1.6cm) button to center top of frame where indicated with red dot, then glue a smaller button on top.

5. Glue acrylic stones to center of each button.

6. Center and glue stitched frame over front of acrylic frame. •

COLOR KEY
Yards	Medium Weight Yarn
8 (7.4m)	■ Skipper blue #848
5 (4.6m)	⁄ White #1 Backstitch
	○ Attach smaller button
	● Attach ⅝-inch (1.6cm) button

Color numbers given are for Red Heart Classic medium weight yarn Art. E267

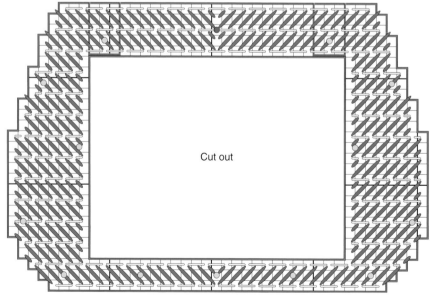

Buttons & Stripes Purse Frame Front
41 holes x 27 holes
Cut 1

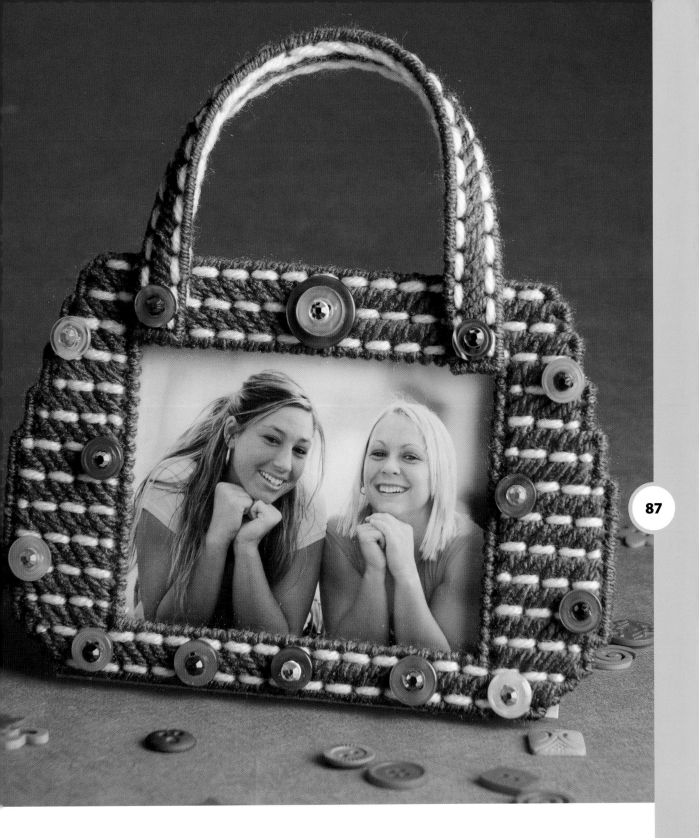

Buttons & Stripes Purse Frame Handle
51 holes x 3 holes
Cut 1

DESIGNS TO MAKE IN A DAY

Fridgie Clips

You'll never forget those important reminders on the fridge again when they're clipped to this set of four eye-catching critters.

Designs by Christina Laws

INSTRUCTIONS

1. Cut plastic canvas according to graphs (this page and pages 89 and 95), carefully cutting out hole in pig's tail.

2. Stitch and Overcast cat, dog and pig pieces following graphs, working Straight Stitches on dog ears. Work Backstitches on cat and dog muzzles while Overcasting.

3. Stitch and Overcast frog pieces following graphs, working uncoded background on body and head pieces with green Continental Stitches and red Straight Stitches on tongue. Work light green Smyrna Cross Stitches over Continental Stitches on body. Work red Backstitches on head.

4. Glue eyes to frog head and to dog, cat and pig bodies where indicated on graphs.

5. Using photo as a guide through step 6, glue ears and muzzles to dog and cat. Glue ears and snout to pig. Glue tongue to frog head, then glue head to frog.

6. Glue one magnetic strip to back of each body. Matching colors, glue clothespins to lower part of bodies. •

GRAPHS CONTINUED ON PAGE 95

SKILL LEVEL
Beginner

SIZES
Cat: 4⅛ inches W x 3¾ inches H (10.5cm x 9.5cm)

Dog: 3¾ inches W x 3⅝ inches H (9.5cm x 9.2cm)

Pig: 3¼ inches W x 3¼ inches H (8.3cm x 8.3cm)

Frog: 2¾ inches W x 3¼ inches H (7cm x 8.3cm)

MATERIALS
- ½ sheet 7-count plastic canvas
- Plastic canvas yarn as listed in color key
- #16 tapestry needle
- 8 miniature plastic spring clothespins: 2 yellow, 2 blue, 2 pink and 2 green
- 8 (5mm) movable eyes
- 4 (1½-inch) lengths magnetic strip
- Hot-glue gun

88

Fridgie Cat Ears
3 holes x 4 holes each
Cut 1 set

Fridgie Cat Muzzle
5 holes x 4 holes
Cut 1

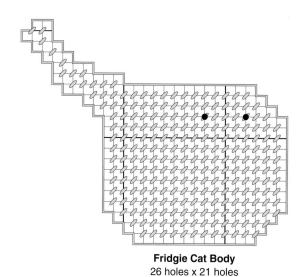

Fridgie Cat Body
26 holes x 21 holes
Cut 1

COLOR KEY	
CAT	
Yards	**Plastic Canvas Yarn**
4 (3.7m)	☐ Yellow
1 (1m)	☐ White
1 (1m)	☐ Pink
	⁄ Pink Backstitch
	● Attach eye

COLOR KEY
FROG

Yards	Plastic Canvas Yarn
1 (1m)	☐ Light green
1 (1m)	■ Red
4 (3.7m)	Uncoded background on body and head are green Continental Stitches
✦	Green Overcast
✦	Red Backstitch and Straight Stitch
●	Attach eye

Fridgie Frog Tongue
3 holes x 3 holes
Cut 1

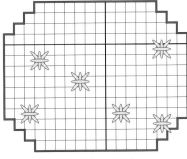

Fridgie Frog Body
18 holes x 14 holes
Cut 1

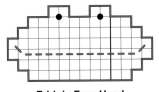

Fridgie Frog Head
14 holes x 7 holes
Cut 1

Fridgie Dog Muzzle
5 holes x 4 holes
Cut 1

COLOR KEY
DOG

Yards	Plastic Canvas Yarn
4 (3.7m)	☐ Light blue
1 (1m)	■ Blue
✦	Blue Backstitch and Straight Stitch
●	Attach eye

Fridgie Dog Ear
3 holes x 4 holes
Cut 2

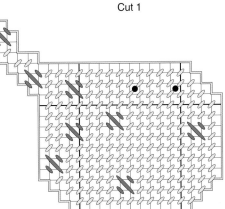

Fridgie Dog Body
24 holes x 20 holes
Cut 1

DESIGNS TO MAKE IN A DAY

Spring Flowers Wall Art

Welcome the warm breeze and beautiful blossoms of spring with this quick-to-stitch wall hanging.

Design by Robin Petrina

INSTRUCTIONS

1. Cut plastic canvas according to graphs.

2. Using spring green, stitch and Overcast letters and leaves following graphs, working Straight Stitch on each leaf when background stitching is completed.

3. Stitch and Overcast one flower following graph. Stitch and Overcast one each of remaining flowers replacing cherry red with yellow, pumpkin, medium purple, grenadine and delft blue.

4. Using photo as a guide throughout, arrange flowers in desired color sequence, glue together from top to bottom. Glue leaves in place. Glue letters to center of flowers spelling "SPRING."

5. Hang as desired. •

SKILL LEVEL
Beginner

SIZE
7¼ inches W x 21½ inches H (18.4cm x 54.6cm)

MATERIALS
- 1 sheet 7-count plastic canvas
- Red Heart Classic medium weight yarn Art. E267 as listed in color key
- Red Heart Super Saver medium weight yarn Art. E300 as listed in color key
- #16 tapestry needle
- Hot-glue gun

90

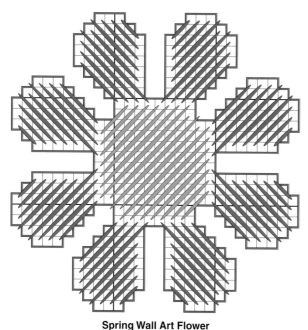

Spring Wall Art Flower
28 holes x 28 holes
Cut 6
Stitch 1 as graphed
Stitch 1 each replacing cherry red
with yellow, pumpkin, medium purple,
grenadine and delft blue

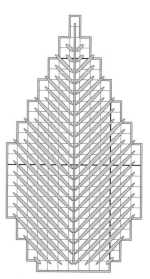

**Spring Flowers Wall Art
Leaf**
13 holes x 24 holes
Cut 3

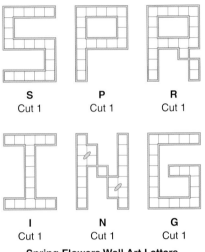

S	P	R
Cut 1	Cut 1	Cut 1

I	N	G
Cut 1	Cut 1	Cut 1

Spring Flowers Wall Art Letters
5 holes x 7 holes each
Cut 1 each

COLOR KEY

Yards	Medium Weight Yarn
6 (5.5m)	Yellow #230
6 (5.5m)	Pumpkin #254
6 (5.5m)	■ Cherry red #319
8 (7.4m)	■ Cafe #360
6 (5.5m)	Medium purple #528
12 (11m)	■ Spring green #672
6 (5.5m)	Grenadine #730
6 (5.5m)	Delft blue #885
╱	Spring green #672 Straight Stitch

Color numbers given are for Red Heart
Classic medium weight yarn Art. E267
and Super Saver medium weight yarn
Art. E300

Handy Home Helpers

These bright and cheerful note keepers are perfect to leave on the counter top or give as gifts.

Designs by Gina Woods

SKILL LEVEL
Beginner

SIZES
Sunflower and Watermelon Heart: 3¼ inches W x 3½ inches H x ⅞ inches D (8.3cm x 8.9cm x 2.2cm), including clothespins

Tropical Fish: 3½ inches W x 3½ inches H x ⅞ inches D (8.9cm x 8.9cm x 2.2cm), including clothespin

MATERIALS
- ⅔ sheet 7-count plastic canvas
- Medium weight yarn as listed in color key
- 6-strand embroidery floss as listed in color key
- #16 tapestry needle
- 3 (3⅜-inch/8.6cm-long) spring wooden clothespins
- 4mm black bead
- Hand-sewing needle
- Hot-glue gun

INSTRUCTIONS

1. Cut plastic canvas according to graphs (this page and page 94).

2. Stitch and Overcast watermelon heart base as graphed. Stitch and Overcast sunflower base replacing pink with pale yellow and deep pink with bright yellow. Stitch and Overcast tropical fish base replacing pink with very light sea green and deep pink with medium sea green.

3. Stitch and Overcast remaining pieces following graphs, working uncoded areas with Continental Stitches as follows: sunflower with pumpkin, tropical fish with yellow-orange and watermelon heart with deep pink.

4. When background stitching is completed, work Lazy Daisy Stitches on sunflower where indicated, using 1 strand bright yellow and 2 strands dark yellow.

5. For tropical fish, work white yarn Straight Stitch at eye. Using 2 plies black floss, work remaining embroidery on fish and fin. For eye, attach bead to fish with hand-sewing needle and black floss.

6. For seeds on watermelon heart, work black yarn Straight Stitches over deep pink Continental Stitches.

ASSEMBLY

1. Use photo as a guide throughout assembly. Glue one clothespin to center back of each base so the squeezing end is about ¼-inch (0.6cm) above bottom edge and clipping end extends above top edge about ¼-inch (0.6cm).

2. Glue leaves behind sunflower at corners, then center and glue sunflower and leaves to front of yellow base.

3. Glue fin to fish, then center and glue fish to front of sea green base.

4. Center and glue watermelon heart to front of pink base. •

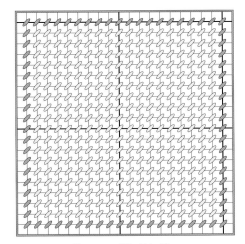

Message Clip Trio Base
21 holes x 21 holes
Cut 3
Stitch 1 as graphed for
watermelon heart
Stitch 1 for sunflower, replacing
pink with pale yellow and
deep pink with bright yellow
Stitch 1 for tropical fish, replacing
pink with very light sea green
and deep pink with medium sea green

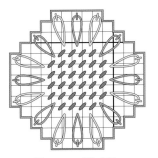

**Message Clip Trio
Sunflower**
13 holes x 13 holes
Cut 1

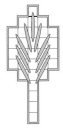

**Message Clip Trio
Sunflower Leaf**
5 holes x 11 holes
Cut 4

COLOR KEY		
SUNFLOWER		
Yards	**Medium Weight Yarn**	
5 (4.6m)	Bright yellow	
4 (3.7m)	Pale yellow	
3 (2.8m)	▢ Leaf green	
1 (1m)	▨ Dark brown	
2 (1.9m)	Uncoded background on sunflower is pumpkin Continental Stitches	
	╱ Pumpkin Overcast	
	◉ Bright yellow (1-strand) Lazy Daisy Stitch	
1 (1m)	◉ Dark yellow (2-strand) Lazy Daisy Stitch	

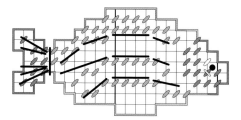

**Message Clip Trio
Tropical Fish**
21 holes x 10 holes
Cut 1

**Message Clip Trio
Tropical Fish Fin**
5 holes x 3 holes
Cut 1

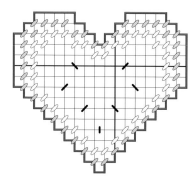

**Message Clip Trio
Watermelon Heart**
17 holes x 15 holes
Cut 1

Tiny Frames Trio

CONTINUED FROM PAGE 68

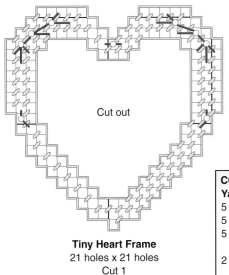

Tiny Heart Frame
21 holes x 21 holes
Cut 1

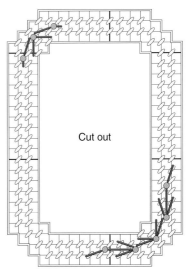

Tiny Rectangle Frame
17 holes x 24 holes
Cut 1

COLOR KEY

Yards	Medium Weight Yarn
5 (4.6m)	☐ Light rose
5 (4.6m)	☐ Light green
5 (4.6m)	☐ Ivory
	6-Strand Embroidery Floss
2 (1.9m)	✐ Green Backstitch and Straight Stitch
1 (1m)	○ White French Knot
1 (1m)	● Light rose French Knot

Fridgie Clips

CONTINUED FROM PAGE 89

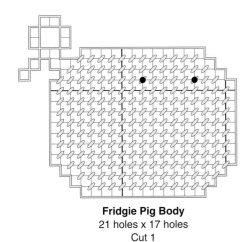

Fridgie Pig Body
21 holes x 17 holes
Cut 1

Fridgie Pig Ears
4 holes x 3 holes each
Cut 1 set

Fridgie Pig Snout
5 holes x 4 holes
Cut 1

COLOR KEY

PIG

Yards	Plastic Canvas Yarn
4 (3.7m)	☐ Pink
1 (1m)	☐ Rose
	● Attach eye

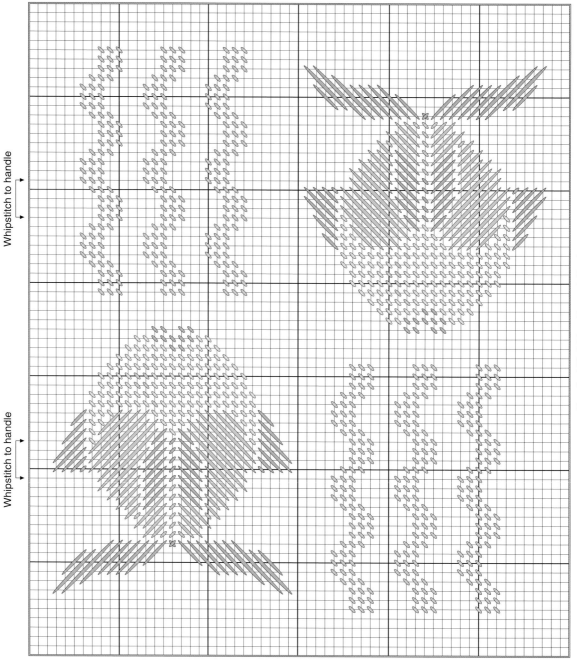

Whipstitch to handle

Whipstitch to handle

Tropical Fish Tote Front & Back
70 holes x 60 holes
Cut 2 from bright green

COLOR KEY	
Yards	**Medium Weight Yarn**
20 (18.3m)	▢ Turquoise
16 (14.7m)	▨ Pink
12 (11m)	▢ Yellow

Button Basket Trio

CONTINUED FROM PAGE 83

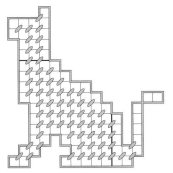

**Button Basket Trio
Playful Cat**
15 holes x 15 holes
Cut 1 from clear

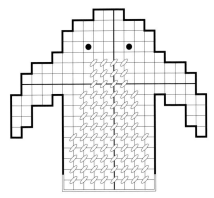

Button Basket Trio Penguin
19 holes x 17 holes
Cut 1 from clear

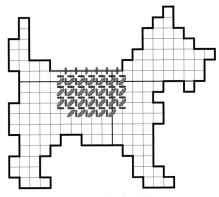

**Button Basket Trio
Scottie Dog**
20 holes x 17 holes
Cut 1 from clear

COLOR KEY

Yards	Medium Weight Yarn
24 (22m)	☐ White
22 (20.2m)	☐ Tan
22 (20.2m)	☐ Light blue
4 (3.7m)	☐ Gray
1 (1m)	■ Red
6 (5.5m)	Uncoded areas on dog and penguin are black Continental Stitches
	✦ Black Overcast
1 (1m)	✦ Burgundy Backstitch
	6-Strand Embroidery Floss
1 (1m)	✦ Kelly green Backstitch
	● Attach movable eye

Holiday Bazaar

Bazaars are filled with holiday ornaments, sit-arounds and other decor items. Get a start on your bazaar stitching or even your holiday decorating with designs for holidays including Halloween, Easter and Christmas.

Gingerbread House Decor

Calorie free, this gingerbread house will add a little sweetness to your home over the holidays.

Design by Ronda Bryce

SKILL LEVEL
Intermediate

SIZE
8¾ inches W x 11¼ inches H (22.2cm x 28.6cm)

MATERIALS
- 1 sheet 7-count plastic canvas
- 6-inch Uniek QuickShape plastic canvas heart
- 6-inch Uniek QuickShape plastic canvas radial circle
- 3 (3-inch) Uniek QuickShape plastic canvas radial circles
- Uniek Needloft plastic canvas yarn as listed in color key
- #16 tapestry needle
- 23 (5mm) white pompoms
- 3 (12 x 10mm) red heart pony beads
- 1¼-inch (3.2cm) white ribbon rose bow
- 11 red glass E beads
- ⅝-inch (1.6cm) round red fashion button with shank
- 5 Favorite Findings Reach for the Stars star buttons #550000485 in pink, yellow, purple, orange and green from Blumenthal Lansing Co.
- Hand-sewing needle
- White, red, green and camel thread

INSTRUCTIONS
1. Cut plastic canvas according to graphs (pages 102, 103 and 104), cutting away blue areas on heart and circles.

2. Following graphs throughout all stitching, stitch and Overcast one gumdrop with fern as graphed. Stitch and Overcast one each of remaining gumdrops with purple, bittersweet, watermelon and yellow.

3. Stitch and Overcast window frames with white. Stitch wreath with fern; Overcast with Christmas green. Stitch and Overcast house, door and hanger.

ASSEMBLY
1. Use photo as a guide throughout assembly. With hand-sewing needle and red thread, sew red fashion button to door for doorknob where indicated on graph.

2. Using white thread throughout and making sure bottom edges are even, center and sew door to unstitched area of gingerbread house. Center window frames over windows and stitch in place.

3. Use red thread to sew one red heart pony bead to center bottom of each window frame; sew remaining red heart pony bead to house where indicated on graph.

4. Use white thread to sew ribbon rose bow to center bottom of wreath. Attach red E beads to wreath as desired with red thread. Sew wreath to door with green thread.

5. Use camel thread to sew gumdrops along bottom of house on both sides of door; sew stars to house over door where indicated on graph.

6. Using white thread through step 7, sew pompoms just below roof of house where indicated on graph. Sew remaining 10 pompoms to gumdrops.

7. Sew ends of hanger behind chimney and roof. •

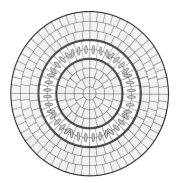

Gingerbread House Wreath
Cut 1 from 3-inch radial circle,
cutting away blue area
Stitch as graphed

Gingerbread House Window Frame
Cut 2 from 3-inch radial circle,
cutting away blue area
Stitch and Overcast with white

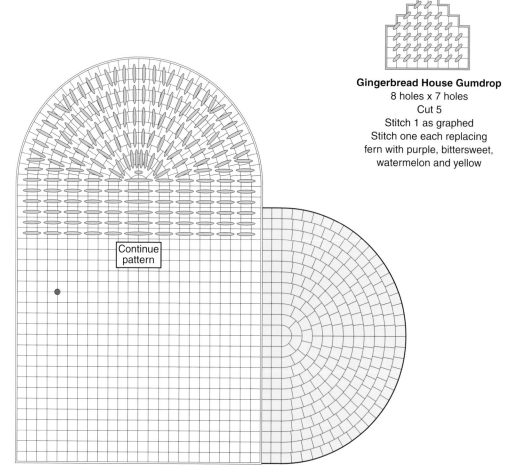

Gingerbread House Gumdrop
8 holes x 7 holes
Cut 5
Stitch 1 as graphed
Stitch one each replacing
fern with purple, bittersweet,
watermelon and yellow

Continue
pattern

Gingerbread House Door
Cut 1 from plastic canvas heart,
cutting away blue area

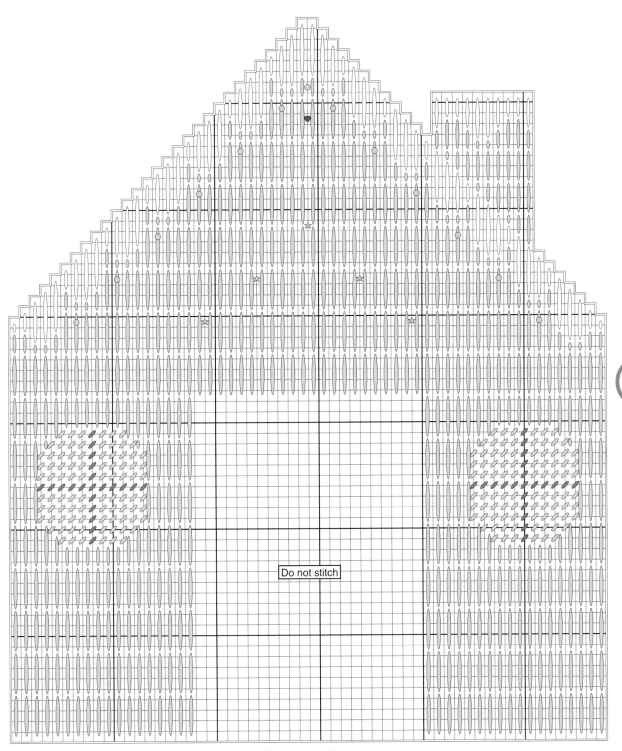

Do not stitch

Gingerbread House
58 holes x 68 holes
Cut 1

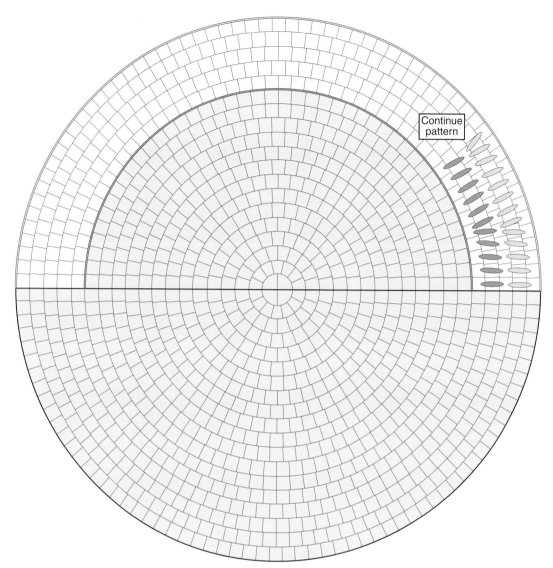

Gingerbread House Hanger
Cut 1 from 6-inch radial circle,
cutting away blue area

Continue
pattern

COLOR KEY	
Yards	**Plastic Canvas Yarn**
1 (1m)	■ Brown #15
3 (2.8m)	☐ Fern #23
3 (2.8m)	☐ Silver #37
2 (1.9m)	☐ Gray #38
13 (11.9m)	☐ White #41
40 (36.6m)	☐ Camel #43
1 (1m)	Purple #46
1 (1m)	Bittersweet #52
1 (1m)	Watermelon #55
7 (6.5m)	☐ Yellow #57
2 (1.9m)	╱ Christmas green #28 Overcast
	● Attach red fashion button
	☆ Attach star button
	♥ Attach red heart pony bead
	○ Attach white pompom

Color numbers given are for Uniek Needloft plastic
canvas yarn.

Gingerbread Goodie Basket

Family and friends will be delighted when you surprise them with this adorable basket filled with their favorite treats.

Design by Gina Woods

SKILL LEVEL
Beginner

SIZE
4⅜ inches W x 5 inches H x 2¾ inches D (11.1cm x 12.7cm x 7cm), including pompoms

MATERIALS
- ½ sheet clear 7-count plastic canvas
- Small amount brown 7-count plastic canvas
- Medium weight yarn as listed in color key
- #16 tapestry needle
- 2 (12 x 10mm) opaque red heart pony beads
- 2 (½-inch/13mm) white iridescent pompoms
- Hand-sewing needle and red thread
- Hot-glue gun

INSTRUCTIONS

1. Cut walls and roof pieces from clear plastic canvas according to graphs. Cut one 21-hole x 15-hole piece from brown plastic canvas for base. Base will remain unstitched.

2. Stitch remaining pieces following graphs, working uncoded backgrounds with medium brown Continental Stitches.

3. Using white, Overcast roof edges and top edges of front, back and side walls from blue dot to blue dot.

4. When background stitching is completed, use 1 ply emerald green to Backstitch swirls on spring green lollipops, 2 plies emerald green to work Lazy Daisy Stitches for holly leaves, 2 plies white to Straight Stitch windowpanes, and 2 plies red to work French Knots for holly berries.

5. Use full strand (4 plies) yarn as follows: pink to Backstitch around doors, white to Straight Stitch lollipop sticks on side walls, medium brown to Straight Stitch along wall edges next to lollipops.

6. Using hand-sewing needle and red thread, attach heart pony beads to doors where indicated on graph.

7. Using white, Whipstitch front and back to sides, being careful not to catch medium brown Straight Stitches in Whipstitching. Using emerald green, Whipstitch front, back and sides to unstitched base.

8. Using photo as a guide throughout, glue roof pieces to front and back. Glue pompoms to peaks of roof pieces where indicated. •

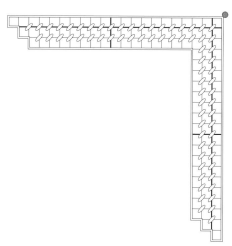

Gingerbread Goodie Basket
Roof
21 holes x 21 holes
Cut 2

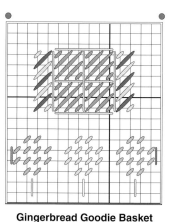

Gingerbread Goodie Basket
Side Wall
15 holes x 17 holes
Cut 2

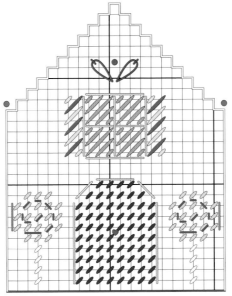

Gingerbread Goodie Basket
Front & Back Wall
21 holes x 27 holes
Cut 2

COLOR KEY	
Yards	**Medium Weight Yarn**
12 (11m)	☐ White
3 (2.8m)	■ Dark brown
2 (1.9m)	☐ Spring green
2 (1.9m)	■ Red
2 (1.9m)	☐ Pink
2 (1.9m)	☐ Gold
1 (1m)	☐ Orange
1 (1m)	☐ Yellow
1 (1m)	☐ Medium lavender
14 (12.9m)	Uncoded backgrounds are medium brown Continental Stitches
3 (2.8m)	╱ Emerald green Whipstitch
	╱ Medium brown (4-ply) Straight Stitch
	╱ White (4-ply) Straight Stitch
	╱ Pink (4-ply) Backstitch
	╱ White (2-ply) Straight Stitch
	╱ Emerald green (1-ply) Backstitch
	ᕲ Emerald green (2-ply) Lazy Daisy Stitch
	● Red (2-ply) French Knot
	♥ Attach heart pony bead
	● Attach pompom

Gingerbread Garland

Add a cheery touch to your mantel this season with a delightfully cheerful garland featuring smiling gingerbread friends.

Design by Robin Petrina

SKILL LEVEL
Beginner

SIZES
Garland: Approximately 32 inches L x 4 inches H, with no swag (81.3cm x 10.2 cm)

Gingerbread Boy & Girl: 3¼ inches W x 4 inches H (8.3cm x 10.2cm)

Candies: 1½ inches W x 2⅝ inches H (3.8cm x 6cm)

Candy Cane: 1⅝ inches W x 3⅜ inches H (4.1cm x 8.6cm)

Wreath: 2 inches W x 2 inches H (5.1cm x 5.1cm)

MATERIALS
- 1 sheet 7-count plastic canvas
- Red Heart Classic medium weight yarn Art. E267 as listed in color key
- Red Heart Super Saver medium weight yarn Art. E300 as listed in color key
- Metallic craft cord as listed in color key
- #16 tapestry needle
- Hot-glue gun

PROJECT NOTE

Use 4 plies medium weight yarn for stitching and embroidery unless otherwise instructed.

INSTRUCTIONS

1. Cut plastic canvas according to graphs (pages 109 and 110).

2. Stitch and Overcast one candy cane as graphed. Reverse remaining candy cane before stitching, reversing direction of stitches.

3. Stitch and Overcast remaining pieces, working uncoded areas on gingerbread boy and girl with warm brown Continental Stitches.

4. When background stitching is completed, work burgundy French Knots and pale rose Cross Stitches. Using 2 plies yarn, work white and burgundy Backstitches and black French Knots. Work white/gold French Knots for buttons.

5. Cut about a 1 yard (1m) length white/gold metallic cord. Thread cord through stitching on back of each piece in following order: gold candy, left-facing candy cane, blue candy, gingerbread boy, wreath, gingerbread girl, gold candy, right-facing candy cane, blue candy.

6. With wreath in center, space pieces about 1 inch (2.5cm) apart. Tie a loop on each end for hanging. Tie a small length of burgundy yarn in a bow and glue to center top of wreath. •

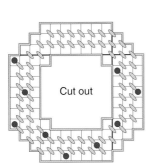

Gingerbread Garland Wreath
13 holes x 13 holes
Cut 1

COLOR KEY	
Yards	**Medium Weight Yarn**
7 (6.5m)	☐ White #311
3 (2.8m)	▨ Cherry red #319
5 (4.6m)	☐ Cornmeal #320
3 (2.8m)	■ Burgundy #376
4 (3.7m)	■ Hunter green #389
2 (1.9m)	▨ Light sage #631
5 (4.6m)	☐ Blue jewel #818
6 (5.5m)	Uncoded areas are warm brown #336 Continental Stitches
	⟋ White #311 (2-ply) Backstitch
	⟋ Burgundy #376 (2-ply) Backstitch
1 (1m)	✖ Pale rose #755 Cross Stitch
1 (1m)	● Black #312 (2-ply) French Knot
	● Burgundy #376 French Knot
	Metallic Craft Cord
2 (1.9m)	◉ White/gold French Knot

Color numbers given are for Red Heart Classic medium weight yarn Art. E267 and Super Saver medium weight yarn Art. E300.

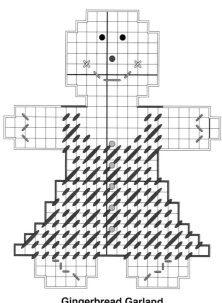

**Gingerbread Garland
Gingerbread Girl**
21 holes x 26 holes
Cut 1

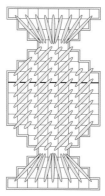

**Gingerbread Garland
Candy Cane**
10 holes x 22 holes
Cut 2
Stitch 1 as graphed
Reverse 1 and work
stitches in reverse

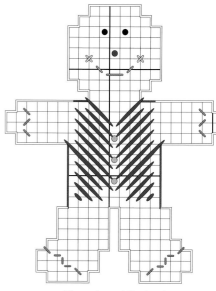

**Gingerbread Garland
Gingerbread Boy**
21 holes x 26 holes
Cut 1

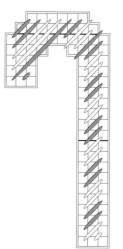

**Gingerbread Garland
Gold Candy**
9 holes x 17 holes
Cut 2

**Gingerbread Garland
Blue Candy**
9 holes x 17 holes
Cut 2

COLOR KEY

Yards	Medium Weight Yarn
7 (6.5m)	☐ White #311
3 (2.8m)	■ Cherry red #319
5 (4.6m)	☐ Cornmeal #320
3 (2.8m)	■ Burgundy #376
4 (3.7m)	■ Hunter green #389
2 (1.9m)	▨ Light sage #631
5 (4.6m)	☐ Blue jewel #818
6 (5.5m)	Uncoded areas are warm brown #336 Continental Stitches
	╱ White #311 (2-ply) Backstitch
	╱ Burgundy #376 (2-ply) Backstitch
1 (1m)	✖ Pale rose #755 Cross Stitch
1 (1m)	● Black #312 (2-ply) French Knot
	● Burgundy #376 French Knot
Metallic Craft Cord	
2 (1.9m)	● White/gold French Knot

Color numbers given are for Red Heart Classic medium weight yarn Art. E267 and Super Saver medium weight yarn Art. E300.

Candy Cane Mini Frame

Add a holiday touch to your fridge with this tiny frame.

Design by Betty Hansen

INSTRUCTIONS

1. Cut plastic canvas according to graphs. Cut one 15-hole x 17-hole piece for frame back. Frame back will remain unstitched.

2. Following graphs throughout, stitch candy cane. Overcast with Striped Overcast, stitching first with white, then red. Stitch frame front; Overcast inside edges.

3. Using white or red yarn, attach candy cane to lower right corner of frame.

4. Whipstitch frame front and back together around side and bottom edges, Overcasting remaining edges at top of frame front while Whipstitching.

5. Adhere magnetic tape to frame back. •

SKILL LEVEL
Beginner

SIZE
2⅞ inches W x 3⅜ inches H (7.3cm x 8.6cm), including candy cane

MATERIALS
- Small amount 7-count plastic canvas
- Medium weight yarn as listed in color key
- #16 tapestry needle
- 1 x 1¼-inch (2.5 x 3.2cm) piece magnetic tape

111

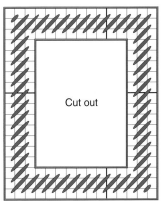

Candy Cane Mini Frame
15 holes x 18 holes
Cut 1

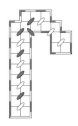

Candy Cane Mini Frame
Candy Cane
6 holes x 10 holes
Cut 1

COLOR KEY	
Yards	Medium Weight Yarn
3 (2.8m)	■ Green glitter
1 (1m)	■ Red
1 (1m)	□ White

Santa Claus Ornament

Jolly ol' St. Nick will add a cheery touch to your holiday decor.

Design by Ronda Bryce

INSTRUCTIONS

1. Cut plastic canvas according to graphs, cutting away gray areas on face circle, hat cuff and hat top.

2. Stitch and Overcast face circle following graph. Stitch and Overcast hat cuff and hat top, leaving blue shaded areas and adjacent edges unstitched.

3. Stitch face, working uncoded areas on white background with white Continental Stitches and uncoded area on pale yellow background with sandstone Continental Stitches; do not Overcast.

4. Center face circle over face; sew in place with hand-sewing needle and white thread.

5. Use photo as a guide through step 6. Using hand-sewing needle and burgundy thread, stitch hat cuff behind face and face circle, then sew hat top behind cuff, slightly off to the side.

6. Using hand-sewing needle and white thread, tack pompom to hat top.

7. Insert ornament hook through hole of hat top at center of assembled Santa. •

SKILL LEVEL
Beginner

SIZE
4⅜ inches W x 6⅛ inches H (11.1cm x 15.6cm)

MATERIALS
- ⅓ sheet 7-count plastic canvas
- 2 (4-inch) Uniek QuickShape plastic canvas radial circles
- 1 (3-inch) Uniek QuickShape plastic canvas radial circle
- Uniek Needloft plastic canvas yarn as listed in color key
- #16 tapestry needle
- 1-inch (25mm) white pompom
- Hand-sewing needle
- White and burgundy thread
- Silver Christmas ornament hook

112

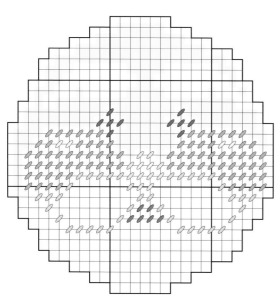

Santa Claus Ornament Face
26 holes x 26 holes
Cut 1

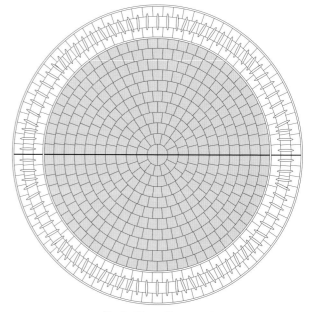

Santa Claus Ornament Face Circle
Cut 1 from 4-inch radial circle, cutting away gray area

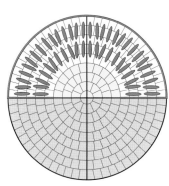

**Santa Claus Ornament
Hat Top**
Cut 1 from 3-inch radial circle,
cutting away gray area
Do not stitch blue shaded area

COLOR KEY	
Yards	**Plastic Canvas Yarn**
1 (1m)	■ Red #01
3 (2.8m)	■ Burgundy #03
2 (1.9m)	■ Lavender #05
1 (1m)	☐ Pink #07
1 (1m)	■ Brown #15
2 (1.9m)	☐ Silver #37
1 (1m)	☐ Eggshell #39
11 (10.1m)	☐ White #41
3 (2.8m)	Uncoded areas on face with pale yellow background are sandstone #16 Continental Stitches
	Uncoded areas on face with white background are white #41 Continental Stitches

Color numbers given are for Uniek Needloft plastic canvas yarn.

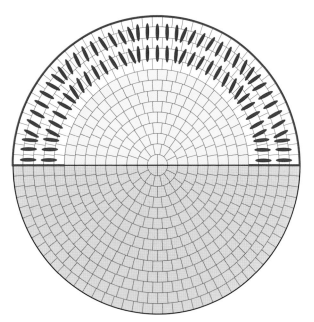

**Santa Claus Ornament
Hat Cuff**
Cut 1 from 4-inch radial circle,
cutting away gray area
Do not stitch blue shaded area

Mini Santa Frame

Add your favorite photo to this fun hat and belt embellished frame to turn anyone into Santa.

Design by Angie Arickx

INSTRUCTIONS

1. Cut plastic canvas according to graphs.

2. Stitch and Overcast pieces following graphs, working red French Knots last.

3. Using photo as a guide, glue holly sprig to hat, then glue hat to acrylic frame top. Glue belt to frame bottom. •

SKILL LEVEL
Beginner

SIZE
3⅛ inches W x 4¾ inches H
(8cm x 12.1cm)

MATERIALS
- ¼ sheet 7-count plastic canvas
- Uniek Needloft plastic canvas yarn as listed in color key
- Uniek Needloft metallic craft cord as listed in color key
- #16 tapestry needle
- 2 x 3-inch (5.1 x 7.6cm) magnetic acrylic photo frame
- Hot-glue gun

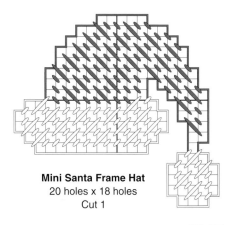

Mini Santa Frame Hat
20 holes x 18 holes
Cut 1

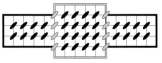

Mini Santa Frame Belt
15 holes x 5 holes
Cut 1

Mini Santa Frame Holly Sprig
4 holes x 4 holes
Cut 1

COLOR KEY

Yards	Plastic Canvas Yarn
1 (1m)	■ Black #00
2 (1.9m)	■ Red #02
1 (1m)	■ Christmas green #28
2 (1.9m)	□ White #41
	● Red #02 French Knot
	Metallic Craft Cord
1 (1m)	▨ Gold #55001

Color numbers given are for Uniek Needloft plastic canvas yarn and metallic craft cord.

Santa Pin

Dress up your favorite jacket or sweater with eye-catching Santa pin. His beaded beard adds a little extra pizzazz.

Design by Alida Macor

INSTRUCTIONS

1. Cut plastic canvas according to graph. Cut felt slightly smaller than Santa.

2. Stitch and Overcast Santa following graph, working uncoded area with pink Continental Stitches.

3. When background stitching is completed, use hand-sewing needle and black thread to attach beads for eyes where indicated on graph.

4. Glue pompom to tip of hat.

5. Cut pearl string beads in 11 lengths with about seven beads in each length.

6. Using photo as a guide, place top of lengths where indicated at blue dots; glue or sew with hand-sewing needle and white thread. If desired, trim off a bead or two along bottom edge to shape beard.

7. Back with felt. Glue or sew pin back to felt. •

SKILL LEVEL
Beginner

SIZE
2¼ inches W x 2⅞ inches H (5.4cm x 7.3cm)

MATERIALS
- Small amount 7-count plastic canvas
- Medium weight yarn as listed in color key
- #16 tapestry needle
- 2 (4mm) round black beads
- 10mm white pompom
- 16 inches (40.6cm) 4mm white pearl string beads
- 1-inch (25mm) pin back
- Small amount adhesive-backed white felt
- Hand-sewing needle
- Black and white (optional) thread
- Craft glue

115

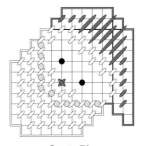

Santa Pin
12 holes x 12 holes
Cut 1

COLOR KEY	
Yards	Medium Weight Yarn
2 (1.9m)	☐ White
1 (1m)	■ Red
1 (1m)	Uncoded area is pink Continental Stitches
	● Attach black bead
	○ Attach pearl string beads

Pocket Santa Ornament

Decorate for the holidays with this darling ornament that features a pocket for a gift card or small gift.

Design by Robin Petrina

SKILL LEVEL
Beginner

SIZE
3½ inches W x 5½ inches H (8.9cm x 14cm)

MATERIALS
- ½ sheet 7-count plastic canvas
- Red Heart Super Saver medium weight yarn Art. E300 as listed in color key
- Darice metallic craft cord as listed in color key
- #16 tapestry needle
- Hot-glue gun

INSTRUCTIONS
1. Cut plastic canvas according to graphs. Pocket back will remain unstitched.

2. Following graphs throughout, stitch pocket front. Stitch and Overcast remaining pieces.

3. When background stitching is completed, use 2 plies to work black French Knots for eyes and gold Backstitches and Running Stitches on pocket front.

4. Overcast top edges of pocket front, then Whipstitch pocket front and back together around side and bottom edges.

5. For hanger, cut desired length of country blue yarn. Thread ends through holes indicated on back piece to inside of pocket; knot ends.

6. Using photo as a guide, glue Santa inside pocket so arms are resting on top edge. Glue beard, then hat in place. Glue star to center of pocket front. •

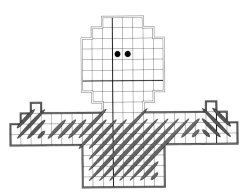

Pocket Santa Ornament
Santa
22 holes x 16 holes
Cut 1

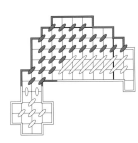

Pocket Santa Ornament
Hat
12 holes x 11 holes
Cut 1

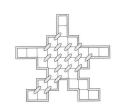

Pocket Santa Ornament
Star
9 holes x 8 holes
Cut 1

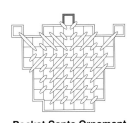

Pocket Santa Ornament
Beard
11 holes x 9 holes
Cut 1

COLOR KEY	
Yards	**Medium Weight Yarn**
3 (2.8m)	☐ White #311
2 (1.9m)	■ Cherry red #319
1 (1m)	■ Paddy green #368
5 (4.6m)	▨ Country blue #382
1 (1m)	Uncoded area on Santa is light coral #327 Continental Stitches
1 (1m)	⁄ Gold #321 (2-ply) Backstitch and Running Stitch
1 (1m)	● Black #312 (2-ply) French Knot
	Metallic Cord
1 (1m)	☐ White/silver #34021-112
	◉ Attach hanger

Color numbers given are for Red Heart Super Saver medium weight yarn Art. E300 and Darice metallic cord.

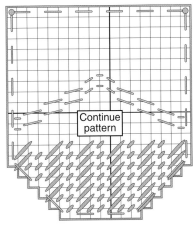

Continue pattern

Pocket Santa Ornament
Pocket Front & Back
18 holes x 20 holes
Cut 2, stitch 1

Rudy Reindeer Ornament

Cute as can be, this adorable reindeer will add Christmas cheer to your home.

Design by Debra Arch

PROJECT NOTE

Use #16 tapestry needle and 2 strands taupe when stitching with yarn. Use #18 tapestry needle and 2 strands when stitching with black metallic ribbon.

INSTRUCTIONS

1. Separate egg halves. Cut through each half vertically according to graphs (page 121), cutting away gray areas.
2. Join halves of one egg top to one egg bottom at connecting edges. Place tape over joining area on inside of egg to secure, making sure to allow room for stitching.
3. Cut back piece from heart and antlers from hexagon according to graphs (page 120), cutting away gray areas.
4. Stitch and Overcast antlers following graph, reversing one antler before stitching. Stitch remaining pieces following graphs. *Note: Each divided stitch at connecting edge on head top and bottom is one complete stitch over connecting*

edge, three holes down on head bottom and four holes up on head top.
5. Thread ends of silver cord through holes indicated on head top to inside of head. Tie ends together in a knot to make a loop for hanging.
6. Using taupe, Whipstitch head front to head back.

FINISHING

1. Use photo as a guide through step 4. Glue antlers to top of head.
2. Wrap bead and silver metallic garlands around green garland, then wrap around head. Trim ends and glue in place, keep silver cord hanger free.
3. Glue on beads, cabochons or buttons for eyes and jingle bell for nose. Apply blush to cheeks with cotton swab.
4. Wrap 1 strand taupe several times around three fingers. Remove from fingers and tie in center. Cut open folded ends. Glue to top of head between antlers. •

SKILL LEVEL
Beginner

SIZE
5½ inches W x 6½ inches H (14cm x 16.5cm), excluding hanger

MATERIALS
- 3-inch-diameter Uniek QuickShape plastic canvas 3-dimensional egg
- 5-inch Uniek QuickShape plastic canvas hexagon
- 6-inch Uniek QuickShape plastic canvas heart
- Red Heart Plush medium weight yarn Art. E719 as listed in color key
- Kreinik ⅛-inch Ribbon as listed in color key
- #16 tapestry needle
- #18 tapestry needle
- 9 inches (22.9cm) thin silver cord
- 24 inches (61cm) 1-inch/2.5cm-wide green garland
- 24 inches (61cm) red bead garland
- 24 inches (61cm) ⅜-inch/1cm-wide silver metallic garland
- 1 inch (2.5cm) silver jingle bell
- 2 (12mm) black beads, cabochons or buttons
- Red blush
- Cotton swab
- Clear packing tape
- Hot-glue gun

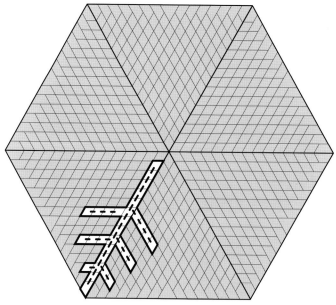

Rudy Reindeer Ornament Antler
Cut 2, reverse 1, from hexagon,
cutting away gray area

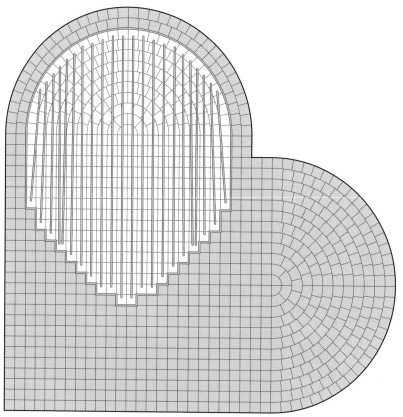

**Rudy Reindeer Ornament
Head Back**
Cut 1 from heart,
cutting away gray area

COLOR KEY

Yards	Medium Weight Yarn
35 (32m)	☐ Taupe #9104 (2 plies)
	⟋ Taupe #9104 (2-ply) Straight Stitch
	¹/₈-Inch Ribbon
11 (10.1)	✁ Black hi lustre #005HL (2-ply) Backstitch
	● Attach silver cord

Color numbers given are for Red Heart Plush medium weight yarn Art. E719 and Kreinik ¹/₈-inch Ribbon.

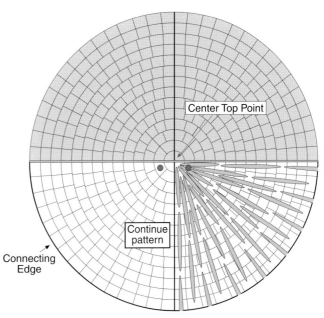

Center Top Point

Continue pattern

Connecting Edge

Rudy Reindeer Ornament
Head Top
Cut 1 egg bottom in half vertically,
cutting away gray area

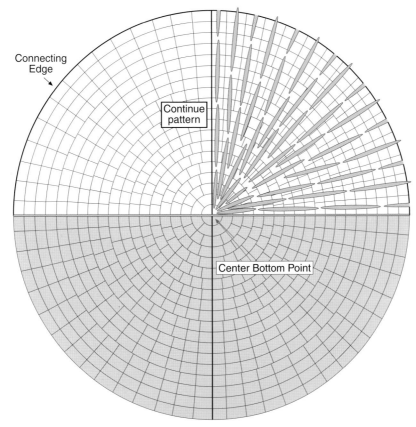

Connecting Edge

Continue pattern

Center Bottom Point

Rudy Reindeer Ornament
Head Bottom
Cut 1 egg top in half vertically,
cutting away gray area

121

Jeweled Stocking Ornaments

Featuring gold beads and rhinestones, these brilliantly colored stockings will add a little extra color to your Christmas tree.

Design by Nancy Valentine

SKILL LEVEL
Beginner

SIZE
3½ inches W x 2½ inches H (8.9cm x 6.4cm)

MATERIALS
- ½ sheet 7-count plastic canvas
- Medium weight yarn as listed in color key
- Metallic cord as listed in color key
- #16 tapestry needle
- 4 (6mm) round gold beads
- 4 (7mm) round faceted rhinestones: blue, green, purple and red
- Fabric glue

INSTRUCTIONS

1. Cut plastic canvas according to graph (page 169).

2. Stitch one stocking as graphed and one replacing red with lime green. Reverse remaining two stockings and stitch one each replacing red with turquoise and violet.

3. When background stitching is completed, work black-gold Straight Stitches on each stocking.

4. Glue beads to tips of stocking where indicated on graph. Glue rhinestones to stockings where indicated on graph, matching color of rhinestone with color of stocking.

5. For hangers, cut four 10-inch (25.4cm) lengths black/gold metallic cord. For each stocking, thread one length through hole indicated on graph. Tie ends together in a knot to form a loop for hanging. Glue knot to back of stocking. •

GRAPH ON PAGE 169

Stocking Treat Holder

Stocking-sized packs of candy fit perfectly in this tiny holiday treat holder.

Design by Deborah Scheblein

INSTRUCTIONS

1. Cut plastic canvas according to graphs (page 169), cutting out hole for hanging at top back of stockings.

2. Following graphs throughout, stitch base. Stitch one stocking as graphed. Reverse remaining stocking and work stitches in reverse.

3. Whipstitch top part of stockings together from blue dot to blue dot, including inside edges. Spread apart bottom portion of stockings, then Whipstitch to base. Overcast remaining edges.

4. Thread yellow ribbon through stocking at cuff line where indicated on graph. Thread bell onto ribbon, then tie in a bow at front seam. •

GRAPHS ON PAGE 169

SKILL LEVEL
Beginner

SIZE
3⅜ inches W x 4⅛ inches H x 1⅛ inches D (35.6cm x 20cm x 2.9cm)

MATERIALS
- ½ sheet 7-count plastic canvas
- Medium weight yarn as listed in color key
- #16 tapestry needle
- 6 inches (15.2cm) ⅛-inch/3mm-wide yellow satin ribbon
- ⅜-inch (9mm) gold jingle bell

123

Snowman Frame

Sized to fit a 4 x 6 frame, you'll love displaying a photo of your loved one in this frosty frame.

Design by Ronda Bryce

INSTRUCTIONS

1. Cut frame and hat from plastic canvas according to graphs (this page and page 170). Cut one 29-hole x 43-hole piece for frame pocket. Pocket will remain unstitched.

2. Stitch and Overcast frame and hat following graphs, working Continental Stitches in uncoded areas as follows: white background with white, green background with holly.

3. When background stitching is completed, work red Straight Stitches for tassel on scarf.

4. Using hand-sewing needle and white thread through step 5, attach pompoms, snowflake buttons, beads for mouth, carrot button for nose and black fashion buttons for eyes and where indicated on graphs.

5. Center frame pocket behind opening of frame. Sew in place around side and bottom edges to stitching on back side, leaving top edge open for insertion of photo.

6. Place hat on top right side of frame, matching blue lines with bottom left side of hat; stitch in place with hand-sewing needle and black thread. •

GRAPHS CONTINUED ON PAGE 170

SKILL LEVEL
Beginner

SIZE
7⅛ inches W x 10½ inches H (18.1cm x 26.7cm)

MATERIALS
- 1 sheet 7-count plastic canvas
- Uniek Needloft plastic canvas yarn as listed in color key
- #16 tapestry needle
- 2 (⅝-inch/1.6cm) round black fashion buttons with shanks
- 1¼-inch carrot button #94739 from JHB International Inc.
- 3 (6–8mm) black glass beads in irregular shapes
- 5 Dress It Up glitter snowflake buttons #1445 from Jesse James & Co.
- 5 (5mm) white pompoms
- Hand-sewing needle
- White and black thread

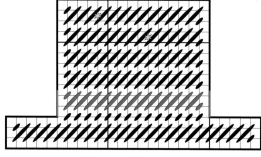

Snowman Frame Hat
25 holes x 14 holes
Cut 1

COLOR KEY	
Yards	**Plastic Canvas Yarn**
5 (4.6m)	■ Black #00
5 (4.6m)	■ Red #01
3 (2.8m)	■ Holly #27
14 (12.9m)	□ Silver #37
4 (3.7m)	Uncoded areas on green background are Christmas green #28 Continental Stitches
13 (11.9m)	Uncoded areas on white background are white #41 Continental Stitches
	╱ Red #01 Straight Stitch
	╱ Christmas green #28 Overcast
	╱ White #41 Overcast
	○ Attach white pompom
	☆ Attach snowflake button
	◆ Attach black bead
	● Attach carrot button
	● Attach black fashion button

Color numbers given are for Uniek Needloft plastic canvas yarn.

Snowman Gift Card Holder

Delight a friend or loved one with a gift card for their favorite store presented in style.

Design by Kristine Loffredo

INSTRUCTIONS

1. Cut plastic canvas according to graphs, carefully cutting away gray areas on snowman.

2. Stitch and Overcast snowman following graph, leaving area indicated unstitched.

3. When background stitching is completed, work black Backstitches and Straight Stitches for mouth; work French Knots for eyes.

4. For fur on cap, work turquoise Turkey Loop Stitches (see Stitch Guide, page 175) in blue shaded area. Cut loops and trim to about ¼-inch (7mm).

5. Stitch and Overcast shoes as graphed. Overcast one nose as graphed. Reverse remaining nose before Overcasting. Whipstitch wrong sides of nose pieces together.

6. Use photo as a guide throughout. Glue nose to face and shoes to bottom of body where indicated on graph. Glue pompom to tip of hat. •

SKILL LEVEL
Intermediate

SIZE
4⅞ inches W x 6¼ inches H x 1 inch D (12.4cm x 15.9cm x 2.5cm), including nose

MATERIALS
- ½ sheet 7-count plastic canvas
- Uniek Needloft plastic canvas yarn as listed in color key
- #16 tapestry needle
- ½-inch (13mm) white tinsel pompom
- Hot-glue gun

126

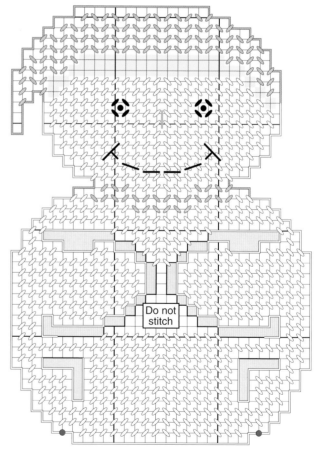

Snowman Gift Card Holder
Snowman
29 holes x 41 holes
Cut 1,
cutting away gray areas

Do not stitch

COLOR KEY

Yards	Plastic Canvas Yarn
4 (3.7m)	■ Black #00
13 (11.9m)	□ White #41
2 (1.9m)	▨ Lilac #45
5 (4.6m)	▨ Turquoise #54
1 (1m)	⁄ Bright orange #58 Overcast
	⁄ Black #00 Backstitch and Straight Stitch
	● Black #00 French Knot
		Attach nose
	● Attach shoe

Color numbers given are for Uniek Needloft plastic canvas yarn.

Snowman Gift Card Holder Shoe
10 holes x 10 holes
Cut 2

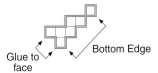

Glue to face

Bottom Edge

Snowman Gift Card Holder Nose
5 holes x 4 holes
Cut 2, reverse 1

Christmas Mouse

Quiet and cute as can be, this tiny mouse ornament looks pretty on your tree or draped from a mantel or shelf.

Design by Betty Hansen

SKILL LEVEL
Intermediate

SIZE
1½ inches W x 9 inches H x 1¼ inches D (3.8cm x 22.9cm x 3.2cm)

MATERIALS
- 1 sheet 7-count plastic canvas
- Medium weight yarn as listed in color key
- 6-strand embroidery floss as listed in color key
- #16 tapestry needle
- Small amount red pearl cotton or embroidery floss

INSTRUCTIONS

1. Cut plastic canvas according to graphs.

2. Stitch pieces following graphs, reversing one body side before stitching and leaving portion indicated at bottom of tail front unworked. Overcast ears and holly.

3. When background stitching is completed, work French Knots for eyes with black embroidery floss. Work green Straight Stitch on holly leaves and red French Knots for berries.

4. Whipstitch wrong sides of tail pieces together around sides and tip of tail from blue dot to blue dot.

5. Using white yarn, tack ears to body sides where indicated with yellow dots.

6. Overcast mouth edges on body sides and base with pink. Whipstitch top edges of mouse body sides together from blue dot to blue dot.

7. Using red pearl cotton or embroidery floss, attach holly where indicated with arrow to inside of mouth.

8. Whipstitch mouse base to bottom edges of body sides from blue dots to green dots. •

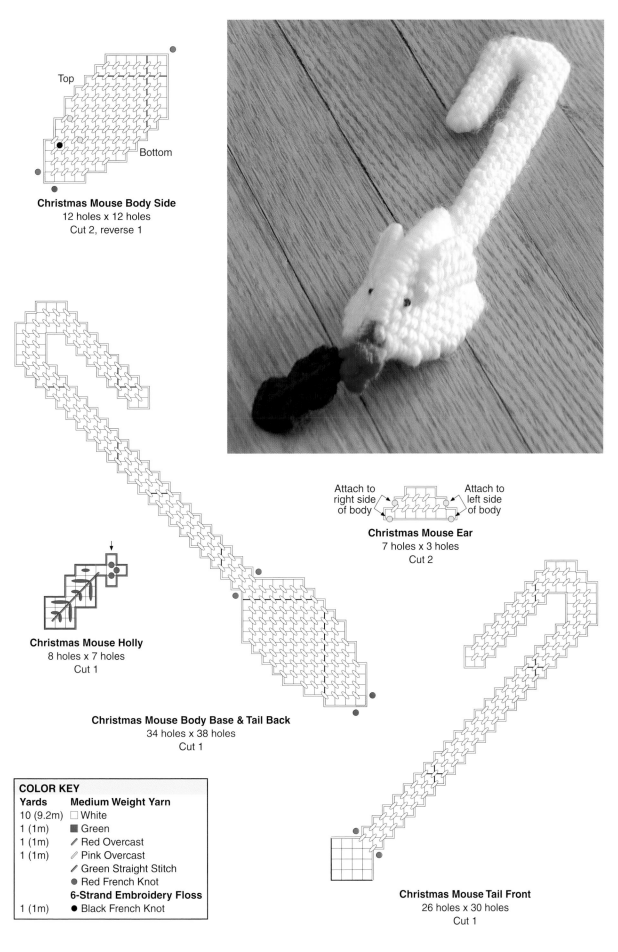

Christmas Mouse Body Side
12 holes x 12 holes
Cut 2, reverse 1

Top

Bottom

Christmas Mouse Holly
8 holes x 7 holes
Cut 1

Christmas Mouse Body Base & Tail Back
34 holes x 38 holes
Cut 1

Attach to right side of body

Attach to left side of body

Christmas Mouse Ear
7 holes x 3 holes
Cut 2

Christmas Mouse Tail Front
26 holes x 30 holes
Cut 1

COLOR KEY

Yards	Medium Weight Yarn
10 (9.2m)	☐ White
1 (1m)	■ Green
1 (1m)	╱ Red Overcast
1 (1m)	╱ Pink Overcast
	╱ Green Straight Stitch
	● Red French Knot
	6-Strand Embroidery Floss
1 (1m)	● Black French Knot

129

Cute & Country Ornaments

Adorned with button accents, these plaid-looking ornaments will add country cheer to your tree.

Designs by Robin Petrina

INSTRUCTIONS

1. Cut plastic canvas according to graphs.

2. Stitch pieces following graphs. Overcast snowman with soft white and tree with light sage.

3. When background stitching and Overcasting are completed, work black, carrot and warm brown embroidery on snowman.

4. Glue star button to middle of tree and blue buttons to snowman where indicated on graphs.

5. For hangers, thread desired length of soft white yarn through hole indicated at top of snowman. Tie ends together in a knot to form a loop for hanging. Repeat with tree, using light sage yarn. •

SKILL LEVEL
Beginner

SIZES
Snowman: 2⅜ inches W x 3⅞ inches H (6cm x 9.8cm), excluding hanger

Tree: 2⅞ inches W x 3⅞ inches H (7.3cm x 9.8cm), excluding hanger

MATERIALS
- ¼ sheet 7-count plastic canvas
- Red Heart Super Saver medium weight yarn Art. E300 as listed in color key
- #16 tapestry needle
- ¾-inch (1.9cm) country red star button
- 2 (½-inch/1.3cm) country blue buttons
- Hot-glue gun

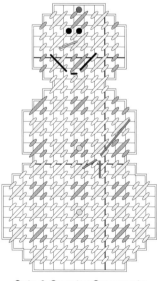

**Cute & Country Ornaments
Snowman**
15 holes x 25 holes
Cut 1

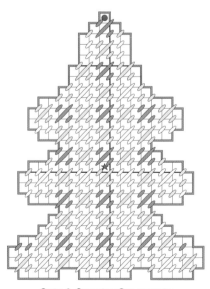

**Cute & Country Ornaments
Tree**
19 holes x 25 holes
Cut 1

COLOR KEY	
Yards	**Medium Weight Yarn**
5 (4.6m)	□ Soft white #316
2 (1.9m)	□ Light blue #381
2 (1.9m)	▨ Country blue #382
2 (1.9m)	▨ Light sage #631
2 (1.9m)	□ Frosty green #661
1 (1m)	╱ Carrot #256 Straight Stitch
1 (1m)	╱ Black #312 Backstitch
1 (1m)	╱ Warm brown #336 Straight Stitch
	● Black #312 French Knot
	○ Attach country blue button
	★ Attach star button
	● Attach hanger

Color numbers given are for Red Heart Super Saver medium weight yarn Art. E300.

Jack-o'-Lantern Can Wrap

Wrap an old coffee can with this fun jack-o'-lantern design and fill it with treats.

Design by Angie Arickx

SKILL LEVEL
Beginner

SIZE
6¼ inches H x 4⅜ inches in diameter (15.9cm x 11.1cm)

MATERIALS
- ½ sheet soft 7-count plastic canvas
- Red Heart Classic medium weight yarn Art. E267 as listed in color key
- Red Heart Super Saver medium weight yarn Art. E300 as listed in color key
- #16 tapestry needle
- 11.5-ounce (326g) coffee can

INSTRUCTIONS

1. Cut plastic canvas according to graph.

2. Stitch piece following graph, overlapping two holes before stitching and working uncoded areas with black Continental Stitches.

3. Overcast stems with emerald and remaining edges with black.

4. Insert coffee can in wrap. •

COLOR KEY

Yards	Medium Weight Yarn
20 (18.3m)	Pumpkin #254
14 (12.9m)	Black #312
3 (2.8m)	Bright yellow #324
8 (7.4m)	Hot red #390
1 (1m)	Emerald green #676
	Uncoded areas are black #312 Continental Stitches

Color numbers given are for Red Heart Classic medium weight yarn Art. E267 and Super Saver medium weight yarn Art. E300.

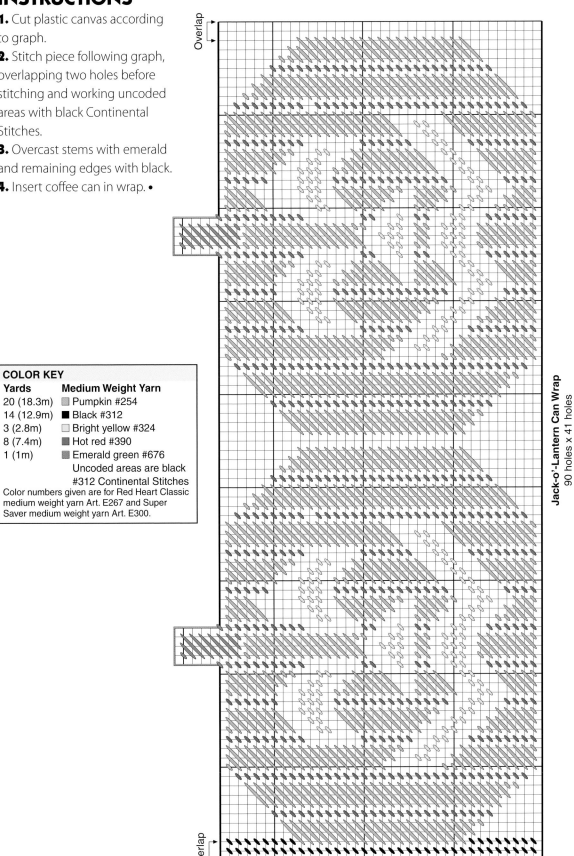

Jack-o'-Lantern Can Wrap
90 holes x 41 holes
Cut 1

133

Ghostly Tree Candleholder

With safety in mind, this spooky decor piece holds a tiny battery-operated tea light.

Design by Darlene Neubauer

SKILL LEVEL
Intermediate

SIZE
4¼ inches W x 5¾ inches H x 2⅞ D (10.8cm x 14.6cm x 7.3cm)

MATERIALS
- 1 sheet 7-count plastic canvas
- Medium weight yarn as listed in color key
- #16 tapestry needle
- Battery-operated tea-light

INSTRUCTIONS

1. Cut plastic canvas according to graphs (pages 136 and 137), cutting out seven holes on front and two holes on each side. One base piece will remain unstitched.

2. Stitch remaining pieces following graphs, working un-coded areas with medium brown Continental Stitches. Overcast inside edges on tree front and sides.

3. Whipstitch tree sides to tree front with royal blue.

4. Using medium brown through step 8, Whipstitch side edges of tea-light holder side together, forming a circle.

5. Place unstitched base under stitched base, then Whipstitch tea-light holder side to circular area on base, Whipstitching along red line and working through all three layers. ***Note:*** *Seam of tea-light holder should face front of base.*

6. Whipstitch base sides to base where indicated on base graph, working through all three layers; tack edges of base sides to tea-light holder side.

7. Whipstitch tree front and sides to base, working through all three layers, then Whipstitch base sides to tree sides.

8. Overcast all remaining edges. Place tea-light in holder. •

Ghostly Tree Candleholder
Tea-Light Holder Side
33 holes x 3 holes
Cut 1

Ghostly Tree Candleholder
Base Side
11 holes x 3 holes
Cut 2

COLOR KEY	
Yards	**Medium Weight Yarn**
17 (15.6m)	☐ Medium brown
4 (3.7m)	■ Royal blue
3 (2.8m)	☐ White
2 (1.9m)	■ Dark brown
1 (1m)	■ Black
	Uncoded areas are medium brown Continental Stitches

Whipstitch
to tree front
left side

Whipstitch
to base side

Ghostly Tree Candleholder
Tree Left Side
14 holes x 31 holes
Cut 1

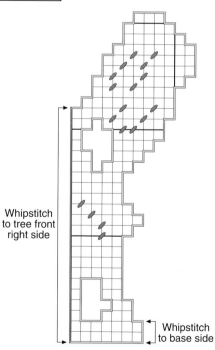

Whipstitch
to tree front
right side

Whipstitch
to base side

Ghostly Tree Candleholder
Tree Right Side
12 holes x 31 holes
Cut 1

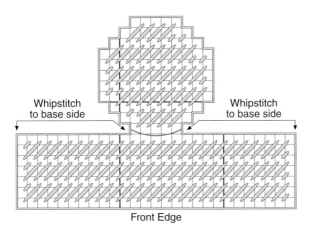

Whipstitch to base side

Whipstitch to base side

Front Edge

Ghostly Tree Candleholder Base
27 holes x 18 holes
Cut 2, stitch 1

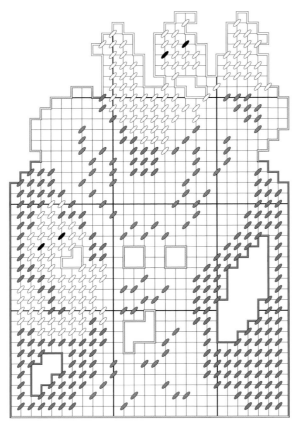

Ghostly Tree Candleholder
Tree Front
27 holes x 38 holes
Cut 1

Wacky Witch Candy Jar

This high-flying witch will greet any little goblins as they take candy from the treat jar!

Design by Mary T. Cosgrove

SKILL LEVEL
Beginner

SIZE
1 inches H x 3⅞ inches in diameter (2.5cm x 4.8cm); fits 3⅝-inch (9.2cm) round lid

MATERIALS
- 1 sheet 7-count plastic canvas
- Uniek Needloft plastic canvas yarn as listed in color key
- Kreinik Fine (#8) Braid as listed in color key
- #16 tapestry needle
- 7mm movable eye
- Jar or container with 3⅝-inch (9.2cm) round lid
- Instant grab craft glue

INSTRUCTIONS
1. Cut plastic canvas according to graphs.

2. Stitch top following graph, working uncoded areas on lid top with bright yellow Continental Stitches.

3. When background stitching is completed, work bittersweet Straight Stitch for mouth and black yarn Straight Stitch between broom head and bristles. Outline features with black braid. Glue movable eye to head where indicated on graph.

4. Stitch lid rim, overlapping 10 holes before stitching. Using bright yellow, Whipstitch lid top to top edge of rim; Overcast bottom edge with black yarn.

5. Using a 1 yard (1m) length of bittersweet, bring yarn from front to back through hole indicated with orange dot. Use a variation of the Running Stitch to weave yarn around rim following graph. Bring yarn out at ending point where indicated with blue dot. Tie in a knot then tie a bow.

6. Place stitched lid over lid of jar or container. •

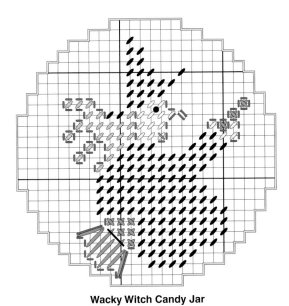

Wacky Witch Candy Jar
Lid Top
25 holes x 25 holes
Cut 1

COLOR KEY	
Yards	**Plastic Canvas Yarn**
11 (10.1m)	■ Black #00
1 (1m)	▨ Fern #23
2 (1.9m)	▨ Bittersweet #52
1 (1m)	☐ Pale peach #56
6 (5.5m)	Uncoded areas on lid top are bright yellow #63 Continental Stitches
	╱ Black #00 Straight Stitch
	╱ Bittersweet #52 Straight Stitch and Running Stitch
	╱ Bright yellow #63 Whipstitch
	Fine (#8) Braid
2 (1.9m)	╱ Black hi lustre #005HL Backstitch
	● Attach movable eye

Color numbers given are for Uniek Needloft plastic canvas yarn and Kreinik Fine (#8) Braid.

Overlap

Wacky Witch Candy Jar
Lid Rim
90 holes x 6 holes
Cut 1

Overlap

139

Sweet 'n' Spooky Treat Bag

The tiny size of this little bag makes it perfect to use as a party favor for a child's Halloween bash.

Design by Cynthia Roberts

SKILL LEVEL
Beginner

SIZE
4⅜ inches W x 7¼ inches H x 1¾ inches D, (11.1cm x 18.4cm x 4.4cm) including handle

MATERIALS
- 1 artist-size sheet 7-count plastic canvas
- Medium weight yarn as listed in color key
- #16 tapestry needle

INSTRUCTIONS

1. Cut plastic canvas according to graphs. **Note:** *Handle section should be 3-holes wide x 57-holes long.* Cut one 27-hole x 11-hole piece for base. Base will remain unstitched.

2. Stitch pieces following graphs, working uncoded areas on front and back with black Continental Stitches and uncoded areas on sides with orange Continental Stitches.

3. When background stitching is completed, work lime green Straight Stitches on front and back and Running Stitches on sides.

4. Overcast handle edges with orange. Using black throughout, Whipstitch front and back to sides; then Whipstitch front, back and sides to unstitched base. Overcast remaining edges. •

140

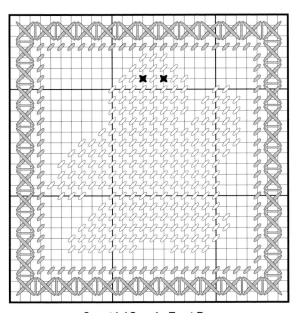

Sweet 'n' Spooky Treat Bag
Front & Back
27 holes x 27 holes
Cut 2

COLOR KEY

Yards	Medium Weight Yarn
13 (11.9m)	■ Black
7 (6.5m)	☐ White
7 (6.5m)	▨ Orange
4 (3.7m)	▨ Lime green
	Uncoded areas on front and back are black Continental Stitches
	Uncoded areas on sides are orange Continental Stitches
╱	Lime green Straight Stitch and Running Stitch

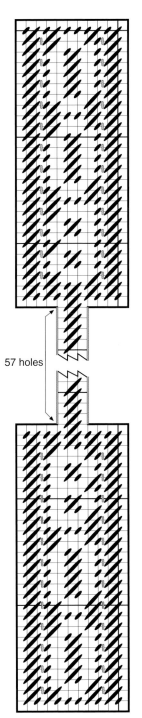

57 holes

141

Sweet 'n' Spooky Treat Bag
Sides & Handle
11 holes x 111 holes
Cut 1

Friendly Bat

This is one bat that's sure not to scare! Try hanging this friendly creature from a fan or mantel for Halloween fun.

Design by Gina Woods

INSTRUCTIONS

1. Cut plastic canvas according to graphs.
2. Cut two fangs from white craft foam using pattern given.
3. Stitch and Overcast head front as graphed; stitch head back entirely with black Continental Stitches; Overcast with black.
4. When background stitching is completed, work lime green Straight Stitch for nose, violet floss Backstitches for mouth and silver metallic thread Straight Stitches for eyebrows on head front only.
5. Work two wings with black Continental Stitches as graphed. Overcast edges. Work violet floss Backstitches on only one of these wings, which will be wing front.
6. Reverse remaining two wings and work with black Continental Stitches; Overcast edges. Work violet Backstitches on only one of these wings, working them in a mirror image of first wing front.

ASSEMBLY

1. Matching edges, glue wrong sides of two wings together. Repeat with remaining two wings.
2. Center wings on wrong side of head back in area below ears, so that violet Backstitches face forward and center edges meet in middle. Glue in place.
3. Glue movable eyes and fangs to face where indicated on graph. •

SKILL LEVEL
Beginner

SIZE
10⅞ inches W x 3¾ inches H (27.6cm x 9.5cm), excluding hanger

MATERIALS
- 1 sheet 7-count plastic canvas
- Medium weight yarn as listed in color key
- DMC 6-strand embroidery floss as listed in color key
- Metallic thread as listed in color key
- #16 tapestry needle
- 2 (10mm) movable eyes
- Small amount 2mm white craft foam
- Hot-glue gun

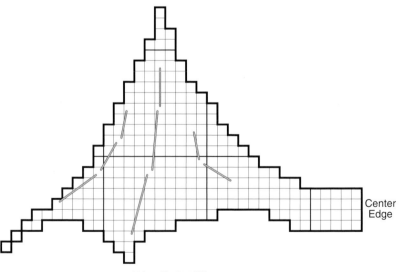

Center Edge

Friendly Bat Wing
35 holes x 24 holes
Cut 4
Stitch 2 as graphed
Work Backstitches on 1 only
Reverse 2 before stitching
Work Backstitches in mirror image on 1 only

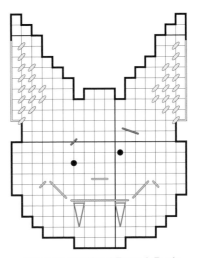

Friendly Bat Fang
Cut 2 from
white craft foam

COLOR KEY

Yards	Medium Weight Yarn
1 (1m)	☐ Peach
22 (20.2m)	Uncoded backgrounds are black Continental Stitches
	✎ Black Overcast
1 (1m)	✎ Lime green Straight Stitch
	6-Strand Embroidery Floss
2 (1.9m)	✎ Violet #553 Backstitch
	Metallic Thread
1 (1m)	✎ Silver Straight Stitch
	● Attach movable eye
	▽ Attach fang

Color number given is for DMC 6-strand embroidery floss.

Friendly Bat Head Front & Back
17 holes x 22 holes
Cut 2
Stitch head front as graphed
Stitch head back entirely
with black Continental Stitches

Gobble Gobble

Set your table in style this Thanksgiving by creating this napkin ring and place-card holder duo for your guests.

Designs by Gina Woods

INSTRUCTIONS

Turkey Motif

1. For each turkey, cut one body, one head and five feathers from plastic canvas according to graphs.

2. Using patterns given, for each turkey, cut one beak from orange craft foam and one wattle from red felt.

3. Stitch and Overcast bodies and heads, working uncoded backgrounds on heads with camel Continental Stitches.

4. For each turkey, stitch and Overcast one feather with red as graphed. Stitch and Overcast two each of remaining feathers with orange and yellow.

5. When background stitching is completed, Straight Stitch eyes with 4-plies black yarn; Backstitch eyebrows with 1 ply black yarn.

6. Using photo as a guide, glue one head to each body at a slight angle and feathers to top back side of body, placing red feather in center. Glue wattle below eyes, then glue beak on top of wattle. Glue single end of paper clip to top back side of center red feather on one turkey.

Napkin Ring

1. Cut one napkin ring according to graph.

2. Stitch ring following graph, overlapping three holes before stitching. Overcast edges.

3. Allow ring to find its natural bottom, then glue turkey without paper clip to ring so that napkin goes in horizontally.

Place-Card Holder

1. Cut one base according to graph. Cut one 19-hole x 13-hole piece for front and one 19-hole x 15-hole piece for back.

2. Work front and back with cream Continental Stitches. Stitch one row of cream Continental Stitches on base where indicated on graph, leaving remaining area unworked.

3. Using cream through step 4, Whipstitch wrong side of back to right side of base where indicated on graph.

4. Whipstitch wrong side of front to right side of base at green line. Whipstitch front and back together along top edges. Overcast remaining edges.

5. Center and glue turkey with paper clip to front, resting bottom edge of turkey on shelf at front of holder.

6. Write desired name on card stock with fine-point pen. Insert card stock in paper clip. •

SKILL LEVEL
Beginner

SIZES
Napkin Ring: 4⅜ inches W x 3⅜ inches H x 1⅞ inches D (11.1cm x 8.6cm x 4.8cm)

Place Card: 4⅜ inches W x 3⅜ inches H x 2 inches D (11.1cm x 8.6cm x 5.1cm)

MATERIALS
- ½ sheet 7-count plastic canvas
- Medium weight yarn as listed in color key
- #16 tapestry needle
- Small amount 2mm-thick orange craft foam
- Small amount red felt
- #1 size silver paper clip
- 3 x 1½-inch (7.6 x 3.8cm) piece white card stock
- Fine-point pen in desired color
- Hot-glue gun

Gobble Gobble Head
8 holes x 8 holes
Cut 1 for each turkey

Gobble Gobble Tail Feather
5 holes x 11 holes
Cut 5 for each turkey
Stitch 1 as graphed
Stitch 2 each with orange and yellow

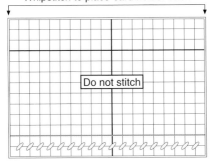

Whipstitch to place-card holder back

Do not stitch

**Gobble Gobble
Place-Card Holder Base**
19 holes x 13 holes
Cut 1

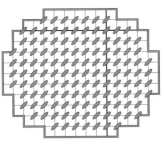

Gobble Gobble Body
15 holes x 12 holes
Cut 1 for each turkey

Gobble Gobble Wattle
Cut 1 for each turkey
from red felt

Gobble Gobble Beak
Cut 1 for each turkey
from orange craft foam

COLOR KEY

Yards	Medium Weight Yarn
13 (11.9m)	☐ Cream
3 (2.8m)	▨ Medium brown
2 (1.9m)	Yellow
2 (1.9m)	Orange
1 (1m)	■ Red
1 (1m)	☐ White
2 (1.9m)	Uncoded backgrounds on heads are camel Continental Stitches
	╱ Camel Overcast
1 (1m)	╱ Black (4-ply) Straight Stitch
	╱ Black (1-ply) Backstitch

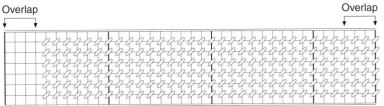

Overlap   Overlap

Gobble Gobble Napkin Ring
36 holes x 7 holes
Cut 1

HOLIDAY BAZAAR

Autumn Leaves Welcome

Brightly colored leaves will warmly welcome your guests as the seasons change.

Design by Deborah Scheblein

SKILL LEVEL
Beginner

SIZE
14 inches W x 7⅞ inches H
(35.6cm x 20cm)

MATERIALS
- 2 sheets 7-count plastic canvas
- Medium weight yarn as listed in color key
- #16 tapestry needle
- Black cloth-covered wire
- Pencil

INSTRUCTIONS

1. Cut plastic canvas according to graphs (this page and pages 148 and 149), cutting out hanger hole on front and back. Back will remain unstitched.

2. Stitch front following graph, working uncoded background with Aran fleck Continental Stitches.

3. Whipstitch front and back together with burgundy.

4. Stitch and Overcast leaves and acorns following graphs. When background stitching is completed, work brown Straight Stitches for veins in leaves.

5. For stems, cut six 2–3¼-inch (5.1–8.3cm) lengths black cloth-covered wire. Fold each in half and twist two or three times. Glue ends of one length each behind leaves A, B, C and D where indicated with arrows. Bend wire slightly.

6. Using photo as a guide through step 7, glue leaves and acorns around edges of welcome sign.

7. Cut two 6-inch (15.2cm) lengths wire. Wrap each around pencil to curl. Slide curls off pencil and glue to sign. •

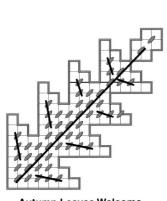

**Autumn Leaves Welcome
Leaf E**
15 holes x 15 holes
Cut 4

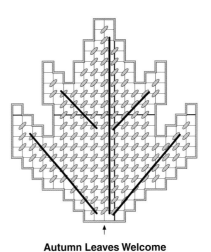

**Autumn Leaves Welcome
Leaf A**
18 holes x 19 holes
Cut 2

COLOR KEY	
Yards	**Medium Weight Yarn**
10 (9.2m)	■ Burgundy
9 (8.3m)	■ Bronze
6 (5.5m)	□ Yellow-orange
2 (1.9m)	■ Red
2 (1.9m)	□ Yellow
36 (33m)	□ Copper
	Uncoded background is Aran fleck Continental Stitches
	╱ Dark brown Straight Stitch

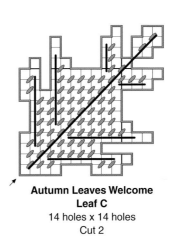

**Autumn Leaves Welcome
Leaf C**
14 holes x 14 holes
Cut 2

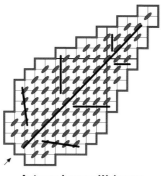

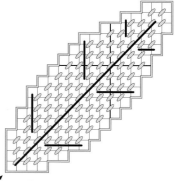

**Autumn Leaves Welcome
Leaf B**
15 holes x 15 holes
Cut 1

**Autumn Leaves Welcome
Leaf D**
16 holes x 16 holes
Cut 1

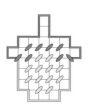

**Autumn Leaves Welcome
Acorn B**
7 holes x 6 holes
Cut 2

**Autumn Leaves Welcome
Acorn A**
7 holes x 8 holes
Cut 2

COLOR KEY	
Yards	**Medium Weight Yarn**
10 (9.2m)	■ Burgundy
9 (8.3m)	■ Bronze
6 (5.5m)	□ Yellow-orange
2 (1.9m)	■ Red
2 (1.9m)	□ Yellow
36 (33m)	□ Copper
	Uncoded background is Aran fleck Continental Stitches
	✁ Dark brown Straight Stitch

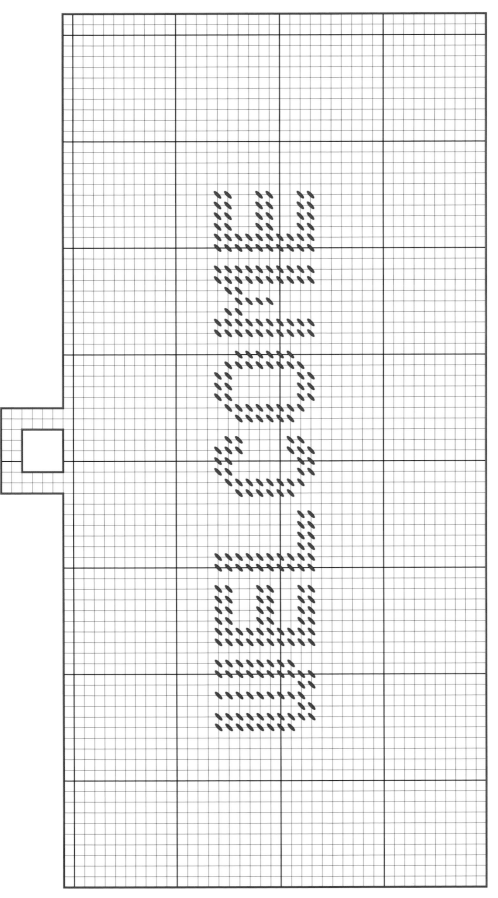

Autumn Leaves Welcome
Sign Front & Back
82 holes x 47 holes
Cut 2
Do not stitch back

149

Autumn Corn

Welcome the cooler temperatures of fall with this decorative piece stitched in harvest colors.

Design by Ronda Bryce

INSTRUCTIONS

1. Cut plastic canvas according to graphs (pages 152 and 153).

2. Stitch and Overcast pieces following graphs, working uncoded background on autumn corn panel with eggshell Continental Stitches and leaving center area on background unstitched as indicated.

3. When background stitching is completed, work dark royal Running Stitches on autumn corn panel.

4. Insert ends of orange ribbon from back to front through holes indicated on autumn corn panel. Tie in a bow on front, trimming ends as desired.

5. Using hand-sewing needle and eggshell thread, center panel over unstitched area on background and Whipstitch in place.

6. Using photo as a guide through step 7, use tangerine yarn to Cross Stitch buttons to corners of background.

7. Center wire star on top edge of background, then tack bottom points of star in place with dark royal. •

SKILL LEVEL
Beginner

SIZE
7½ inches W x 12⅛ inches H (19.1cm x 30.8cm)

MATERIALS
- 2 sheets 7-count plastic canvas
- Uniek Needloft plastic canvas yarn as listed in color key
- #16 tapestry needle
- 18 inches (45.7cm) ¼-inch/7mm-wide orange satin ribbon
- 2 (1¼-inch/3.2cm) Favorite Findings Country buttons #550000497 each in red and yellow from Blumenthal Lansing Co.
- Uniek 5-inch wire star
- Hand-sewing needle
- Eggshell thread

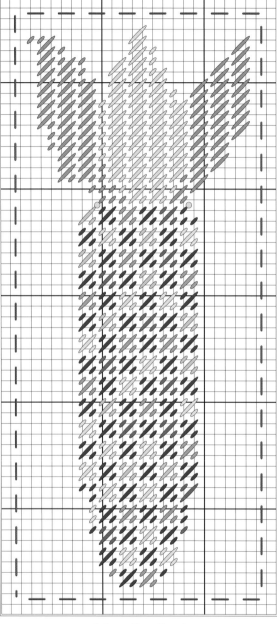

Autumn Corn Panel
27 holes x 58 holes
Cut 1

COLOR KEY

Yards	Plastic Canvas Yarn
6 (5.5m)	■ Red #01
7 (6.5m)	☐ Tangerine #11
6 (5.5m)	☐ Pumpkin #12
3 (2.8m)	☐ Sandstone #16
3 (2.8m)	☐ Camel #43
32 (29.3m)	■ Dark royal #48
6 (5.5m)	■ Bittersweet #52
6 (5.5m)	☐ Yellow #57
20 (18.3m)	Uncoded background on Indian corn panel is eggshell #39 Continental Stitches
	⁄ Eggshell #39 Overcast
	⁄ Dark royal #48 Running Stitch
	⊙ Attach orange ribbon

Color numbers given are for Uniek Needloft plastic canvas yarn.

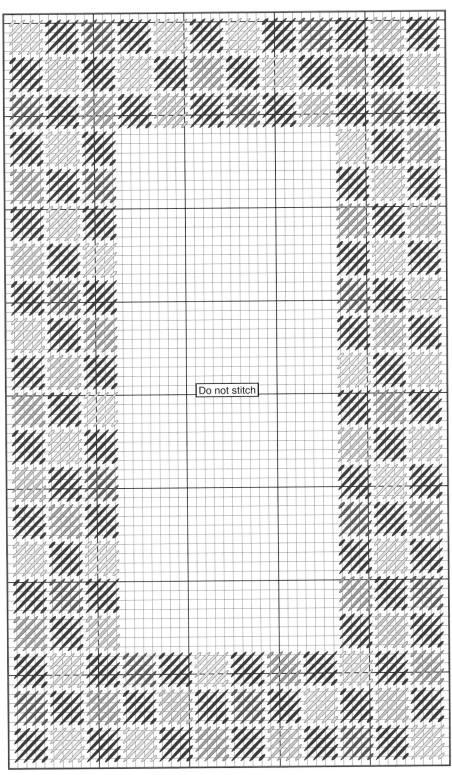

Do not stitch

Autumn Corn Background
49 holes x 81 holes
Cut 1

St. Patrick's Day Shamrock Pin

Add a little green to your outfit this St. Patrick's Day with this quick-and-easy design.

Design by Sandra Miller Maxfield

INSTRUCTIONS

1. Cut plastic canvas according to graph.

2. Stitch and Overcast piece following graph, working uncoded areas with holly Continental Stitches.

3. When background stitching is completed, Backstitch mouth with black and complete nose with a lavender Straight Stitch.

4. Tie satin ribbon in a bow, trimming ends as desired; glue to top of stem (see photo). Glue eyes above nose where indicated on graph. Glue pin back to back of shamrock. •

154

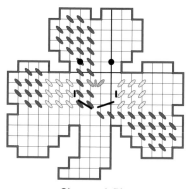

Shamrock Pin
17 holes x 16 holes
Cut 1

COLOR KEY	
Yards	**Plastic Canvas Yarn**
1 (1m)	▨ Lavender #05
1 (1m)	☐ Pink #07
5 (4.6m)	■ Holly #27
	Uncoded areas are holly #27 Continental Stitches
1 (1m)	╱ Black #00 Backstitch
	╱ Lavender #05 Straight Stitch
	● Attach movable eye
Color numbers given are for Uniek Needloft plastic canvas yarn.	

Pot o' Shamrocks

Fill this tiny container with chocolate gold coins or other goodies for a little bit of Irish luck.

Design by Mary T. Cosgrove

INSTRUCTIONS

1. Cut plastic canvas according to graphs (pages 156 and 157), cutting away gray areas on 4-inch radial circles.

2. Stitch pot side following graph, overlapping five holes before stitching. Stitch rim side; Whipstitch short edges together with holly.

3. Stitch pot base, rim bottom and rim top following graphs. Overcast inside edge of rim top with holly.

4. Using gold metallic craft cord through step 5, with wrong sides facing, Whipstitch top edge of rim side outside edge of rim top. Again with wrong sides facing, Whipstitch bottom edge of rim side to outside edge of rim bottom.

5. Whipstitch pot base to bottom edge of pot. Whipstitch inside edge of rim bottom to top edge of pot. •

SKILL LEVEL
Intermediate

SIZE
3⅝ inches H x 4½ inches in diameter (9.2cm x 11.4cm)

MATERIALS
- 1 sheet 7-count plastic canvas
- 2 (4-inch) Uniek QuickShape plastic canvas radial circles
- Uniek Needloft plastic canvas yarn as listed in color key
- Uniek Needloft metallic craft cord as listed in color key
- #16 tapestry needle

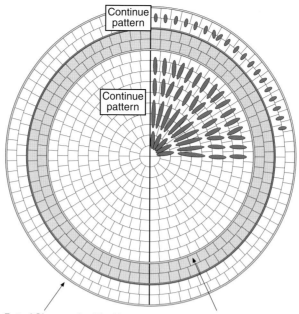

Pot o' Shamrocks Rim Top
Cut 1 from 4-inch radial circle,
cutting away gray area

Pot o' Shamrocks Pot Base
Cut 1 from 4-inch radial circle,
cutting away gray area

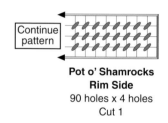

**Pot o' Shamrocks
Rim Side**
90 holes x 4 holes
Cut 1

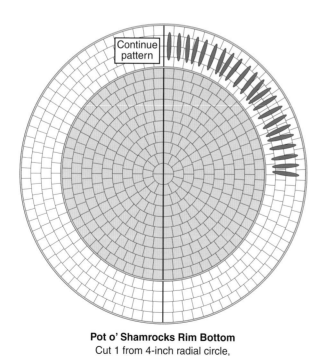

Pot o' Shamrocks Rim Bottom
Cut 1 from 4-inch radial circle,
cutting away gray area

COLOR KEY

Yards	Plastic Canvas Yarn
18 (16.5m)	■ Holly #27
13 (11.9m)	Uncoded areas are white #41 Continental Stitches
	Metallic Craft Cord
8 (7.4m)	▢ Gold #55001

Color numbers given are for Uniek Needloft
plastic canvas yarn and metallic craft cord.

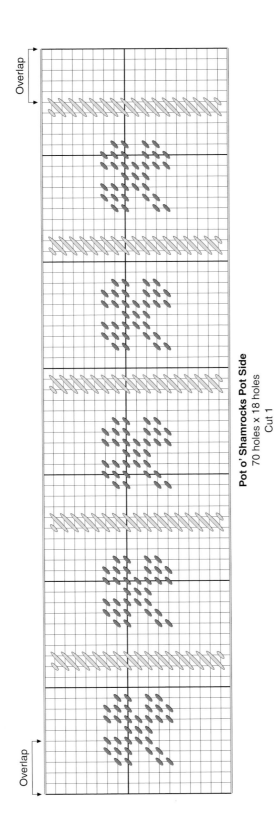

Pot o' Shamrocks Pot Side
70 holes x 18 holes
Cut 1

Bunny Gift Card Holder

Give a gift that they're sure to love this Easter with a gift card presented in this adorable bunny holder.

Design by Kristine Loffredo

INSTRUCTIONS

1. Cut plastic canvas according to graphs, carefully cutting away gray areas on bunny.

2. Stitch and Overcast bunny following graph, leaving area indicated unstitched. Work cinnamon Backstitches on muzzle when background stitching is completed.

3. Stitch and Overcast one large flower with bright pink and one replacing bright pink with bright purple. Stitch and Overcast small flower with bright blue. Do not Overcast center of flowers with fern at this time.

4. Stitch and Overcast bow, leaving stitches at arrows unworked at this time. Overcast nose.

5. Working through both layers, attach large flowers to bunny where indicated, stitching over center edges of flower with fern. Repeat with small flower.

6. Using yellow and working through both layers, attach bow to bunny (yellow dots on bunny graph) with stitches indicated at arrows on bow graph.

7. Glue nose in place where indicated with bright pink lines. •

SKILL LEVEL
Intermediate

SIZE
4¾ inches W x 7 inches H (12.1cm x 17.8cm), including flowers

MATERIALS
- ½ sheet 7-count plastic canvas
- Uniek Needloft plastic canvas yarn as listed in color key
- #16 tapestry needle
- Hot-glue gun

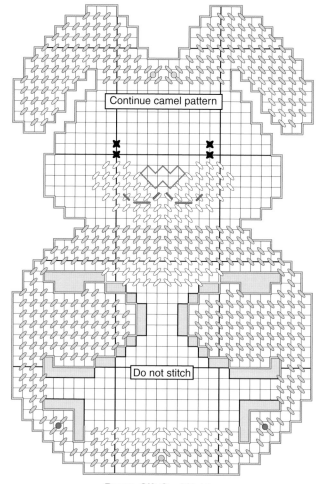

Continue camel pattern

Do not stitch

Bunny Gift Card Holder
Bunny
29 holes x 44 holes
Cut 1,
cutting away gray areas

COLOR KEY

Yards	Plastic Canvas Yarn
1 (1m)	■ Black #00
1 (1m)	☐ Pink #07
2 (1.9m)	☐ White #41
19 (17.4m)	☐ Camel #43
1 (1m)	☐ Yellow #57
1 (1m)	☐ Bright blue #60
2 (1.9m)	■ Bright pink #62
2 (1.9m)	Bright purple #64
1 (1m)	✏ Cinnamon #14 Backstitch
1 (1m)	✏ Fern #23 Overcast
	● Attach large flower
	◐ Attach small flower
	○ Attach bow

Color numbers given are for Uniek Needloft
plastic canvas yarn.

Bunny Gift Card Holder
Nose
3 holes x 3 holes
Cut 1

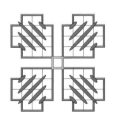

Bunny Gift Card Holder
Large Flower
9 holes x 9 holes
Cut 2
Stitch 1 as graphed
Stitch 1 replacing bright
pink with bright purple

Bunny Gift Card Holder
Small Flower
7 holes x 7 holes
Cut 1

Bunny Gift Card Holder
Bow
7 holes x 7 holes
Cut 1

HOLIDAY BAZAAR

Easter Cross Treat Holder

Instead of hiding eggs, try giving Easter gifts of wrapped candy presented in this pretty holder.

Design by Deborah Scheblein

INSTRUCTIONS

1. Cut plastic canvas according to graphs.

2. Overcast one small flower with yellow as graphed, Overcast one each of remaining small flowers with white, lavender, deep pink and light blue.

3. Stitch and Overcast one large flower with yellow. Stitch and Overcast remaining large flower with lavender.

4. Stitch crosses and base following graphs.

5. Whipstitch top part of crosses together from arrow to arrow. Spread apart bottom portion of crosses, then Whipstitch to base. Overcast remaining edges.

6. Using photo as a guide, glue large lavender flower to center of crossbar. Glue remaining flowers to grass at foot of cross. Glue one pearl to center of each flower. •

160

SKILL LEVEL
Beginner

SIZE
2⅜ inches W x 4⅛ inches H x 1¼ inches D (6cm x 10.5cm x 3.2cm)

MATERIALS
- ½ sheet 7-count plastic canvas
- Medium weight yarn as listed in color key
- #16 tapestry needle
- 7 (3mm) white pearls

**Easter Cross Treat Holder
Small Flower**
3 holes x 3 holes
Cut 5
Overcast 1 as graphed
Overcast 1 each with
white, lavender, deep
pink and light blue

**Easter Cross Treat Holder
Large Flower**
3 holes x 3 holes
Cut 2
Stitch 1 as graphed
Stitch 1 with lavender

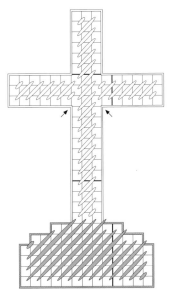

**Easter Cross Treat Holder
Cross**
15 holes x 26 holes
Cut 2

161

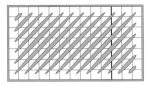

**Easter Cross Treat Holder
Base**
13 holes x 7 holes
Cut 1

COLOR KEY

Yards	Medium Weight Yarn
3 (2.8m)	☐ White
2 (1.9m)	▦ Medium green
1 (1m)	☐ Yellow
1 (1m)	Lavender
1 (1m)	Deep pink
1 (1m)	Light blue
	○ Attach pearl bead

Easter Door Hanger

Display a spiritual message of love this Easter when you create this brightly colored wall hanging.

Design by Mary T. Cosgrove

INSTRUCTIONS

1. Cut plastic canvas according to graph (page 171), cutting away hole between cross and sun.

2. Cut felt slightly smaller than plastic canvas piece.

3. Stitch and Overcast following graph, working white Straight Stitches between letters where indicated.

4. For hanger, wrap wire around pencil to coil. Wrap ends around edges where indicated, then wrap ends around wire to secure.

5. Glue felt to back of stitched piece. •

GRAPH ON PAGE 171

SKILL LEVEL
Intermediate

SIZE
10⅝ inches W x 7⅞ inches H (27cm x 20cm), including hanger

MATERIALS
- 1 sheet 7-count plastic canvas
- Red Heart Classic medium weight yarn Art. E267 as listed in color key
- Red Heart Kids medium weight yarn Art. E711 as listed in color key
- #16 tapestry needle
- 9½ inches (24.1cm) 22-gauge icy blue fizzy Fun Wire from Toner Plastics Inc.
- Pencil
- 1 sheet stiffened white felt
- Fabric glue

163

Star-Spangled Sam

Show your patriotic pride with this delightful Uncle Sam decor piece.

Design by Robin Petrina

PROJECT NOTE

Use 4 plies medium weight yarn for stitching and embroidery unless otherwise instructed.

INSTRUCTIONS

1. Cut plastic canvas according to graphs (this page and page 172).

2. Stitch and Overcast pieces following graphs.

3. When background stitching is completed, work white Straight Stitches for eye highlights. Use 2 plies black to work Backstitches around eyes.

4. Use photo as a guide through step 5. For beard, glue large stars to head over beard area following beard placement diagram (page 172). Glue mustache between eyes and beard.

5. Glue small stars to hat brim, then glue hat brim to head over hat and face seam.

6. Hang as desired. •

GRAPHS CONTINUED ON PAGE 172

SKILL LEVEL
Beginner

SIZE
8⅛ inches W x 11⅝ inches H
(20.6cm x 29.5cm)

MATERIALS
- 1½ sheets 7-count plastic canvas
- Red Heart Super Saver medium weight yarn Art. E300 as listed in color key
- Darice metallic craft cord as listed in color key
- #16 tapestry needle
- Hot-glue gun

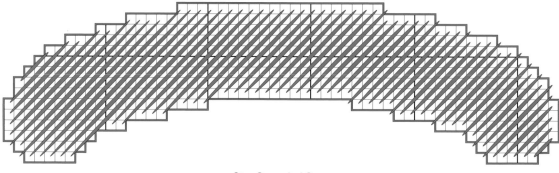

**Star-Spangled Sam
Hat Brim
54 holes x 15 holes
Cut 1**

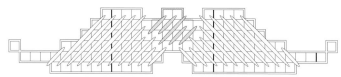

**Star-Spangled Sam Mustache
32 holes x 6 holes
Cut 1**

COLOR KEY	
Yards	**Medium Weight Yarn**
33 (30.2m)	☐ White #311
1 (1m)	■ Black #312
7 (6.5m)	■ Cherry red #319
6 (5.5m)	☐ Light coral #327
1 (1m)	☐ Rose pink #372
8 (7.4m)	■ Royal #385
	✎ White #311 Straight Stitch
	✐ Black #312 Backstitch
	Metallic Cord
5 (4.6m)	☐ White/silver #34021-112

Color numbers given are for Red Heart Super Saver medium weight yarn Art. E300 and Darice metallic cord.

Patriotic Picnic Set

Enjoy a summer picnic with this three-piece set stitched in classic quilt block motifs.

Designs by D.K. Designs

INSTRUCTIONS

Can Cozy

1. Cut can cozy from clear plastic canvas according to graph (page 168). Cut one 60-hole x 20-hole piece from red plastic canvas for lining.

2. Cut away five outermost rows of holes from 4-inch plastic canvas radial circle for base. Base will remain unstitched.

3. Stitch cozy following graph, overlapping three holes before stitching.

4. Overlap four holes of red lining, then stitch overlapped area together with dark red Continental Stitches.

5. Insert red lining in stitched cozy; Whipstitch together with dark blue along top edge. Whipstitch unstitched base to bottom edge of cozy with dark blue.

Coasters

1. Cut four of each coaster from clear plastic canvas according to graphs (page 168). Two pieces for each coaster will remain unstitched and be used for backing.

2. Stitch pieces following graphs. Whipstitch one backing to each stitched coaster with dark blue.

Napkin Holder

1. Cut four holder front and back pieces from clear plastic canvas according to graph (page 168). Two pieces will remain unstitched and be used for backing.

2. Cut the following from clear plastic canvas: two 29-hole x 9-hole pieces for base top and bottom, two 29-hole x 6-hole pieces for base front and back, and two 9-hole x 6-hole pieces for base ends. Base top and bottom will remain unstitched.

3. Stitch holder front and back following graph. Whipstitch one unstitched backing to each with dark blue.

4. Using dark blue throughout, Continental Stitch base front, back and ends. Whipstitch base pieces together, leaving one end open. Fill with aquarium gravel, then Whipstitch remaining end closed.

5. Center and glue wrong sides of holder front and back to right sides of base front and back, making sure bottom edges are even. •

SKILL LEVEL
Beginner

SIZES
Can Cozy: 3¼ inches W x 3 inches in diameter (8.3cm x 7.6cm)

Coasters: 4½ inches W x 3⅞ inches H (11.4cm x 9.8cm)

Napkin Holder: 4½ inches W x 3⅞ inches H x 1⅞ inches D (11.4cm x 9.8cm x 4.8cm)

MATERIALS
- 2 sheets clear 7-count plastic canvas
- ½ sheet red 7-count plastic canvas
- 4-inch Uniek QuickShape plastic canvas circle
- Medium weight yarn as listed in color key
- #16 tapestry needle
- 1 cup aquarium gravel
- Hot-glue gun

COLOR KEY

Yards	Medium Weight Yarn
50 (45.7m)	■ Dark blue
40 (36.6m)	░ Light blue
30 (27.5m)	■ Dark red
25 (22.9m)	□ Off-white

Patriotic Picnic Set
Coaster B
29 holes x 25 holes
Cut 4, stitch 2, from clear

Overlap

Overlap

Patriotic Picnic Set
Can Cozy
63 holes x 21 holes
Cut 1 from clear

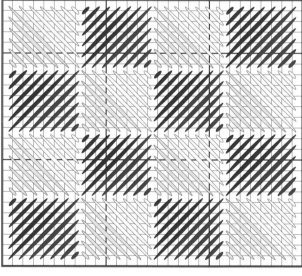

Patriotic Picnic Set
Coaster A
29 holes x 25 holes
Cut 4, stitch 2, from clear

Patriotic Picnic Set
Napkin Holder Front & Back
29 holes x 25 holes
Cut 4, stitch 2, from clear

168

Jeweled Stocking Ornaments

CONTINUED FROM PAGE 122

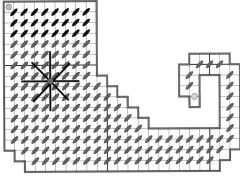

COLOR KEY

Yards	Medium Weight Yarn
4 (3.7m)	■ Red
4 (3.7m)	Lime green
4 (3.7m)	Turquoise
4 (3.7m)	Violet
	Metallic Cord
8 (7.4m)	■ Black/gold
	✦ Black/gold Straight Stitch
	○ Attach gold bead
	● Attach rhinestone
	○ Attach hanger

Jeweled Stocking
23 holes x 16 holes
Cut 4
Stitch 1 as graphed
Stitch 1 replacing red with lime green
Reverse 2, stitch 1 each replacing
red with turquoise and violet

Stocking Treat Holder

CONTINUED FROM PAGE 123

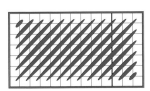

**Stocking Treat Holder
Base**
13 holes x 7 holes
Cut 1

COLOR KEY

Yards	Medium Weight Yarn
4 (3.7m)	■ Green
3 (2.8m)	□ White
3 (2.8m)	■ Red
	○ Attach ribbon

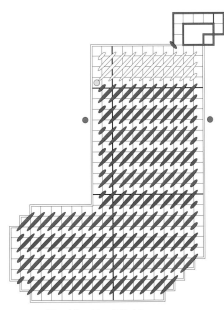

Stocking Treat Holder
21 holes x 27 holes
Cut 2, reverse 1
and work stitches in reverse

169

Snowman Frame

CONTINUED FROM PAGE 124

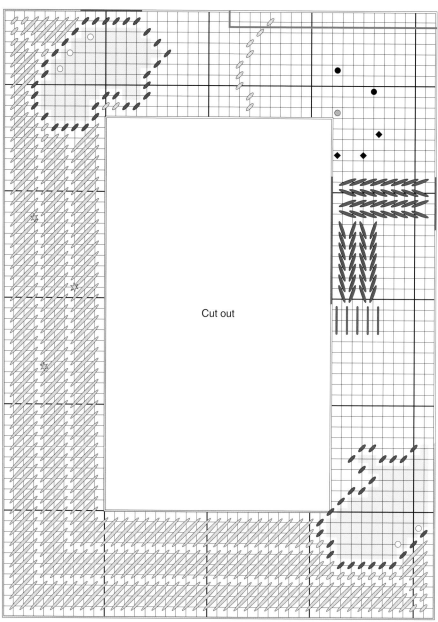

Snowman Frame
42 holes x 57 holes
Cut 1

Easter Door Hanger

CONTINUED FROM PAGE 163

COLOR KEY

Yards	Medium Weight Yarn
8 (7.4m)	☐ White #1
3 (2.8m)	▨ Warm brown #336
6 (5.5m)	☐ Yellow #230
3 (2.8m)	▨ Grenadine #730
3 (2.8m)	▨ Light purple #2358
3 (2.8m)	▨ Lime #2652
	⁄ White #1 Straight Stitch
4 (3.7m)	⁄ Parakeet #513 Overcast
	● Attach wire

Color numbers given are for Red Heart Classic medium weight yarn Art. E267 and Kids medium weight yarn Art. E711.

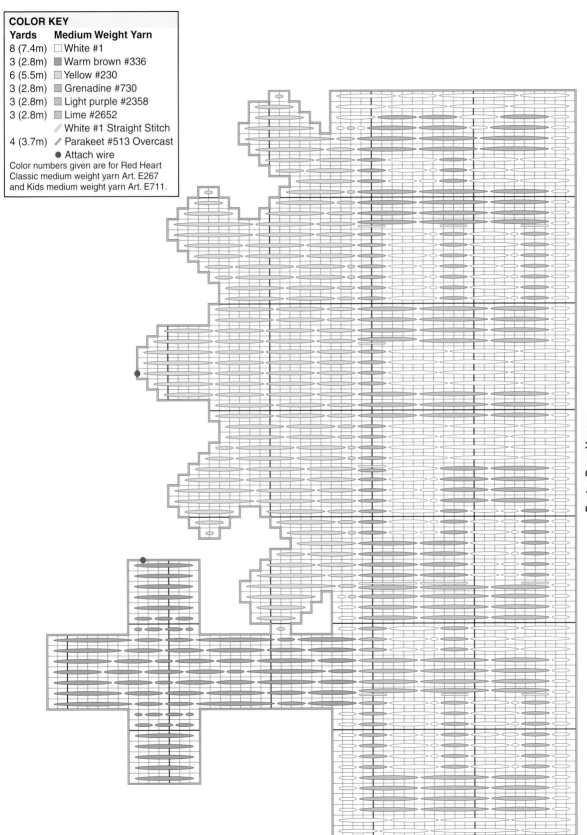

Easter Door Hanger
70 holes x 52 holes
Cut 1

Star-Spangled Sam

CONTINUED FROM PAGE 164

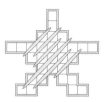

**Star-Spangled Sam
Small Star**
9 holes x 8 holes
Cut 4

**Star-Spangled Sam
Large Star**
19 holes x 20 holes
Cut 8

**Star-Spangled Sam
Beard Placement Diagram**

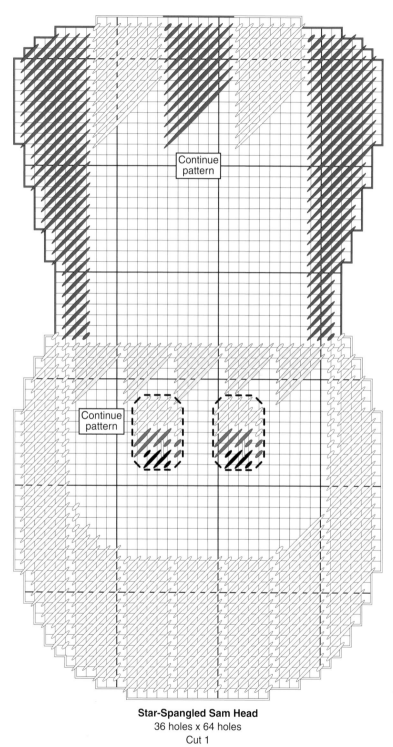

Continue
pattern

Continue
pattern

Star-Spangled Sam Head
36 holes x 64 holes
Cut 1

COLOR KEY	
Yards	**Medium Weight Yarn**
33 (30.2m)	☐ White #311
1 (1m)	■ Black #312
7 (6.5m)	▨ Cherry red #319
6 (5.5m)	☐ Light coral #327
1 (1m)	▨ Rose pink #372
8 (7.4m)	■ Royal #385
	⁄ White #311 Straight Stitch
	✔ Black #312 Backstitch
Metallic Cord	
5 (4.6m)	☐ White/silver #34021-112

Color numbers given are for Red Heart Super
Saver medium weight yarn Art. E300 and
Darice metallic cord.

Special Thanks

We would like to acknowledge and thank the following designers whose original work has been published in this collection. We appreciate and value their creativity and dedication to designing quality plastic canvas projects!

Debra Arch
Chicken Recipe-Card Holder, Chicken Towel Holder, ID Holders, Kitty Tissue Holder, Rudy Reindeer Ornament

Angie Arickx
Deck of Cards Coasters, Jack-o'-Lantern Can Wrap, Mini Santa Frame

Ronda Bryce
Autumn Corn, Baby Bear Ornaments, Flower Frames, Gingerbread House Decor, Santa Claus Ornament, Snowman Frame

Mary T. Cosgrove
Easter Door Hanger, Peeper Keepers, Pot o' Shamrocks, Wacky Witch Candy Jar

D.K. Designs
Patriotic Picnic Set

Nancy Dorman
Tiny Frames Trio

Betty Hansen
A Gentle Reminder, Candy Cane Mini Frame, Christmas Mouse, Pretty in Pink Box

Christina Laws
Fridgie Clips

Kristine Loffredo
Bunny Gift Card Holder, Snowman Gift Card Holder

Alida Macor
Cat Lover's Bookend, Santa Pin

Sandra Miller Maxfield
St. Patrick's Day Shamrock Pin

Darlene Neubauer
Ghostly Tree Candleholder

Sue Penrod
Autumn Leaf Beverage Tags

Robin Petrina
Bluebird & Robin Sit-Arounds, Cute & Country Ornaments, Gingerbread Garland, Pocket Santa Ornament, Spring Flowers Wall Art, Star-Spangled Sam

Terry Ricioli
Celtic Coasters, Tropical Fish Coasters, Tropical Fish Tote

Cynthia Roberts
Sweet 'n' Spooky Treat Bag, Sunflower Desk Set

Deborah Scheblein
Autumn Leaves Welcome, Camouflage Tissue Holder, Doghouse Coaster Set, Easter Cross Treat Holder, Princess Purse Pack, Stocking Treat Holder

Nancy Valentine
Jeweled Stocking Ornaments

Mary Nell Wall
Buttons & Stripes Purse Frame, Diamonds & Jewels Frame

Kathy Wirth
Gerbera Daisy Cube, Sunny Quilt Tissue Topper

Gina Woods
Beach Umbrellas Frame, Blue Skies Frame, Button Basket Trio, Chicken Napkin Holder, Friendly Bat, Gingerbread Goodie Basket, Gobble Gobble, Handy Home Helpers

173

Stitch Guide

Use the following diagrams to expand your plastic canvas stitching skills. For each diagram, bring needle up through canvas at the red number one and go back down through the canvas at the red number two. The second stitch is numbered in green. Always bring needle up through the canvas at odd numbers and take it back down through the canvas at the even numbers.

BACKGROUND STITCHES

The following stitches are used for filling in large areas of canvas. The Continental Stitch is the most commonly used stitch. Other stitches, such as the Condensed Mosaic and Scotch Stitch, fill in large areas of canvas more quickly than the Continental Stitch because their stitches cover a larger area of canvas.

Continental Stitch

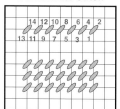

Condensed Mosaic

Alternating Continental

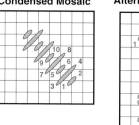

Cross Stitch

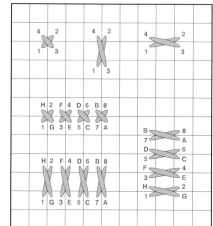

Long Stitch

Scotch Stitch

Slanting Gobelin

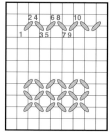

EMBROIDERY STITCHES

These stitches are worked on top of a stitched area to add detail to the project. Embroidery stitches are usually worked with one strand of yarn, several strands of pearl cotton or several strands of embroidery floss.

Lattice Stitch

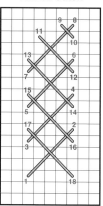

Chain Stitch

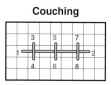

Couching

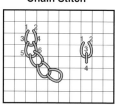

Straight Stitch

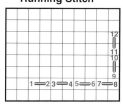

Running Stitch

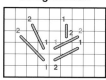

Fly Stitch

Backstitch

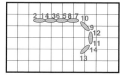

EMBROIDERY STITCHES

French Knot

Bring needle up through canvas. Wrap yarn around needle 1 to 3 times, depending on desired size of knot; take needle back through canvas through same hole.

Lazy Daisy

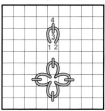

Bring yarn needle up through canvas, then back down in same hole, leaving a small loop. Then, bring needle up inside loop; take needle back down through canvas on other side of loop.

Loop Stitch/Turkey Loop Stitch

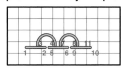

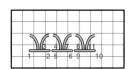

The top diagram shows this stitch left intact. This is an effective stitch for giving a project dimensional hair. The bottom diagram demonstrates the cut loop stitch. Because each stitch is anchored, cutting it will not cause the stitches to come out. A group of cut loop stitches gives a fluffy, soft look and feel to your project.

SPECIALTY STITCHES

The following stitches can be worked either on top of a previously stitched area or directly onto the canvas. Like the embroidery stitches, these too add wonderful detail and give your stitching additional interest and texture.

Satin Stitches

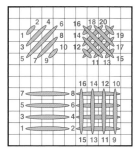

Smyrna Cross

FINISHING STITCHES

Overcast/Whipstitch

Overcasting and Whipstitching are used to finish the outer edges of the canvas. Overcasting is done to finish one edge at a time. Whipstitching is used to stitch two or more pieces of canvas together along an edge. For both Overcasting and Whipstitching, work one stitch in each hole along straight edges and inside corners, and two or three stitches in outside corners.

Lark's Head Knot

The Lark's Head Knot is used for a fringe edge or for attaching a hanging loop.

Buyer's Guide

When looking for a specific material, first check your local craft and retail stores and the Internet. If you are unable to locate a product, contact the manufacturers listed below for the closest retail source in your area or a mail-order source.

Blumenthal Lansing Co.
(563) 538-4211
www.buttonsplus.com

Coats & Clark
(Red Heart, TLC)
(800) 648-1479
www.coatsandclark.com

CPE Inc.
(800) 327-0059
www.cpe-felt.com

Darice
Mail-order source:
Schrock's International
P.O. Box 538
Bolivar, OH 44612
(800) 426-4659

DMC Corp.
(973) 589-0606
www.dmc-usa.com

Elmer's
(800) 848-9400
www.elmers.com

Jesse James & Co. Inc.
Dress It Up Buttons
Distributor:
Shelly's Buttons & More
(888) 811-7441
www.shellysbuttonsandmore.com

JHB International Inc.
(800) 525-9007
www.buttons.com

Kreinik Mfg. Co. Inc.
(800) 537-2166
www.kreinik.com

Toner Plastics Inc.
(413) 789-1300
www.tonercrafts.com

Uniek
Mail-order source:
Annie's Attic
(800) 282-6643
www.anniesattic.com